impact

WORKBOOK 2

SERIES EDITORS
JoAnn (Jodi) Crandall
Joan Kang Shin

NATIONAL GEOGRAPHIC LEARNING

Australia • Brazil • Mexico • Singapore • United Kingdom • United States

Unit 1

Colour Matters

1 **Complete the sentences.** Then fill in the puzzle.

Across

1. Many businesses use the colour blue to ____represent____ them.
2. The colour green often symbolises ________________.
3. In many countries, people think the colour red is ________________.
4. ________________ colours often make us feel happy.
5. Blue jeans are coloured with indigo ________________.

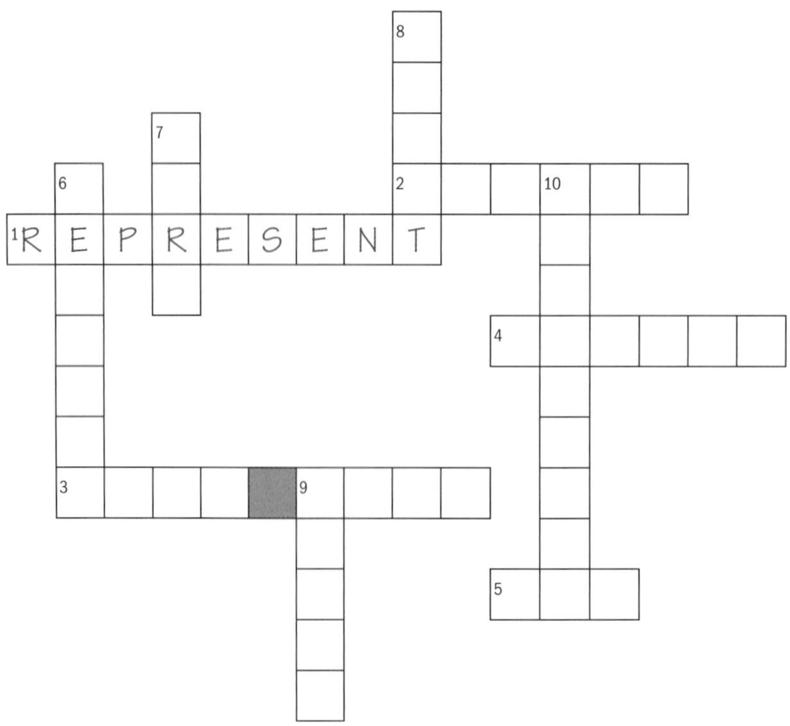

Down

6. In some countries, ________________ dresses are red.
7. Red and yellow are used to ________________ people of danger.
8. When we ________________ someone, we often feel safe with them.
9. Violet is a ________________ purple colour.
10. ________________ vehicles are often red.

2 **Match the word to its definition.** Write the letter on the line.

_____	1. warn	a. to give information or a warning
_____	2. signal	b. to believe in someone or something
_____	3. good luck	c. to say that danger is coming
_____	4. trust	d. something good that happens

3 **Listen.** Circle **T** for *True* or **F** for *False.* 002

1.	T	F	4.	T	F
2.	T	F	5.	T	F
3.	T	F	6.	T	F

4 **Listen again.** Correct the false statements. 003

____

____

____

____

5 **Look at the photos.** Choose two and write a sentence about them. Use a word from the box in each sentence.

signal	represent	danger	flag	luxury	colour-blind	warn

A car like this is a luxury.

____

____

GRAMMAR

Comparatives and superlatives: Comparing two or more things

Adjective	Comparative	Superlative
Green is a **common** colour.	Red is **more common than** purple.	Blue is **the most common** colour.
Fuchsia is a **bright** pink colour.	Hot pink is **brighter than** fuchsia.	Magenta is **the brightest** colour.
Fish that live deep in the sea have **bad** eyesight.	Bats have **worse** eyesight **than** deep-sea fish do.	Moles have **the worst** eyesight.

We use comparatives to compare two things. Use **more** before adjectives that have two or more syllables. Add **-er** to adjectives that have just one syllable. With two-syllable adjectives that end in *y*, both options are possible (*tastier* or *more tasty*). Remember to change *y* to *i*.

With a group of three or more things, we use superlatives to compare one thing in the group to the rest. Superlatives always take ***the***. Use **most** before adjectives that have two or more syllables. Add **-est** to adjectives that have just one syllable. With two-syllable adjectives that end in *y*, both options are possible (*the tastiest* or *the most tasty*). Remember to change *y* to *i*.

Some adjectives are irregular: ***good/better/best*** and ***bad/worse/worst***.

1 **Listen.** Write the letter *C* when you hear a comparative and the letter *S* when you hear a superlative. 004

1. C
2. ____
3. ____
4. ____
5. ____
6. ____

2 **Listen again.** Re-write the comparatives as superlatives and the superlatives as comparatives. 005

1. the best
2. ____________
3. ____________
4. ____________
5. ____________
6. ____________

3 **Fill in the blanks.** Use the adjective, the comparative or the superlative form of the words from the box.

bright	**common**	**depressed**	**light**
nervous	**ordinary**	**relaxed**	**strong**

1. Brighter colours often get ____________________ reactions than lighter ones.
2. Light colours make us feel ____________________ dark colours.
3. That's why pale yellow and pink are ____________________ black in schools and hospitals.
4. Dark colours tend to make people feel ____________________.
5. The colour that makes people ____________________ is red.
6. Orange is one of the ____________________ colours.
7. Pink is a colour that is ____________________ red.
8. A room without colour looks very ____________________.

4 **Write.** Choose at least two colours you really like. Write four sentences comparing the colours and how you feel about them. Use either a comparative or superlative in each sentence.

____

____

____

____

____

____

1 **Listen and read.** As you read, think about the order of events. 006

Colour, Colour, Colour!

'Colour, colour, colour!' are the words of artist and illustrator Eric Carle. Eric is like royalty in the world of children's books. He has written over 70 children's books. His most famous book, *The Very Hungry Caterpillar*, is common on children's bookshelves all over the world. What most people don't know is that Eric makes art for adults, too. A lot of people do not know about Eric's 'ArtArt'. 'ArtArt' is what Eric's work for adults is called. People didn't know about it, because he didn't show it to the public until he was 84 years old!

Like Eric's children's books, his 'ArtArt' is full of bright, vibrant colours. He says that he loves colour so much because he missed it during the war in Germany. Eric was born in Syracuse, New York, in 1929, but moved to Germany with his family when he was six. When he was 10, World War II began. He noticed that all the houses and buildings in his town were painted grey, brown or dark green. It was a sad time, and it seemed like there was no colour anywhere.

At the end of the war, 'when colour came back', Eric explains, 'I just loved it so much. I keep saying that I wish our eyes could see more colour. Colour is a very important part of my work.'

Anyone who has seen Eric's books can see how important colour is to the artist. He paints bright colours on paper, cuts out shapes, and then glues them onto another piece of paper. This is no ordinary method – it is called *collage*. In fact, this method is what led Eric to his 'ArtArt'. He never planned on making art for adults, but when he saw all the extra pieces of colourful paper he had from cutting out shapes, he decided to make something out of them.

Eric's 'ArtArt' includes large collages as well as paintings, sculptures, photographs and even costumes. In all these works, he uses a rainbow of colours – everything from purple to light green to orange. Now that's a lot of colour!

2 **Read.** Then tick **T** for *True* or **F** for *False*. Correct the false statements.

	T	F
1. Eric has created many books for adults.	☐	☐
2. Most people know Eric's 'ArtArt'.	☐	☐
3. *Collage* is a method of gluing coloured pieces of paper together.	☐	☐
4. The colours used during the war represent sadness for Eric.	☐	☐

____

____

3 **Read 'Colour, Colour, Colour!' again.** Use the events below to fill in the order of events and when they happened.

~~**moved to Germany**~~	**showed 'ArtArt' to public**	~~**born**~~
'colour came back'	**World War II began**	

Event	When It Happened
born	1929
moved to Germany	age 6

4 **Write.** You have read about the history of purple and the artist Eric Carle. What is similar about William Perkin's and Eric Carle's experiences while doing their work?

____

____

____

____

____

____

____

____

GRAMMAR

The: Identifying general and specific things

My friend started a new company.
The company is called *Colour Works*.

The moon is glowing orange tonight.

The human eye can see over 10 million colours.

Can you pass me **the** green crayon?

We use the definite article *the* to refer to a specific noun. The noun is specific because

- it was mentioned before or it is known.
- we're referring to it in general.
- there is only one.
- we're providing information that makes it specific.

Use the indefinite article *a/an* to refer to something for the first time (*I bought a bright pink pen.*) or to refer to something that is not specific. (*Do you have a colourful dress for the party?*) You can't use *a/an* with plural nouns.

1 **Read.** Circle the correct word.

1. **The** / **A** back wall of this art room is neon pink.
2. What's **the** / **a** name of this dark blue colour?
3. Our classroom has **a** / **the** colourful work station.
4. **The** / **A** moon is very bright in the night sky.
5. I bought **a** / **the** new pair of shoes. **The** / **A** colour of these shoes is light green.
6. Lucy wore **an** / **the** orange and green scarf. I didn't know she had one.
7. In some countries, seeing **the** / **a** black cat is good luck.

2 **Fill in the blanks.** Use *the* or *a/an*.

1. The sign said to slow down, but Juan did not notice _____ warning.
2. Walking on green grass is _____ luxury for Linda because she lives in the desert.
3. Andi wants to start _____ online company that sells fabric dyes.
4. _____ wedding will be next Saturday afternoon. Ana is so nervous!
5. Have you ever seen violet clouds in _____ sky?
6. _____ French flag on the capitol building is very large.

3 **Read Suki and Jake's blog.** Write your comments and advice. Make sure you use *the* and *a/an* in your response.

Suki and Jake's Design Blog

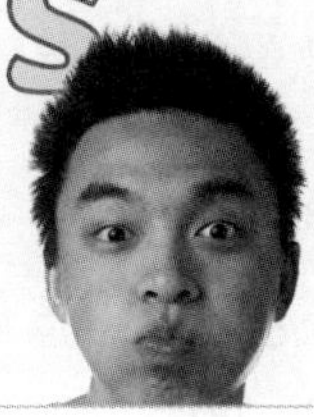

Welcome to our blog! Some of you may have noticed that we want to repaint the school's art room. Mr Lee says he trusts us and gives the students full control. Jake and I started a committee. As leaders of the committee, we are nervous. We will make the final decision, but want to hear from the whole student body.

So far, some of the students say they like the room as it is. They like the bright colours and the fun photographs. But many others say we need a new look.

A common idea among several students is to paint a mural. Everyone can help. The question is, 'What will the mural be?' Another suggestion is that students enter design ideas into a contest. The winner will design the large side wall. And the runner-up will decorate the smaller front and back walls.

So, what will we do? Leave the art room as it is? Paint a mural? Create a contest in which the winners design the walls? Or something else?

Sam

I like the mural idea. It could be of the school flag!

Lucy

I agree that the art room needs a new look. I think the contest is a good idea.

____

____

____

WRITING

A topic sentence introduces the main idea of a paragraph. It says what the paragraph is going to be about. It also makes readers want to know more. The topic sentence is usually the first sentence of the paragraph, but it does not always have to be. It explains:

- what you want to say
- why you are writing

Look at these examples of topic sentences:

In this article, I'm going to discuss the history of the colour orange.
When taking a photograph, it's important to think about light and colour.
Each of the colours and shapes of the South Korean flag represents something specific.
Many people who are colour-blind cannot tell the difference between red and green.

1 Organise.

1. Your topic is *Colour Matters*. Look through Unit 1 in your book to get some ideas about what colours you like, what connections you have to them, and how they make you feel.
2. Now fill in the idea map about the colour you chose to write about. Include the colour, your connection to it, and how it makes you feel.

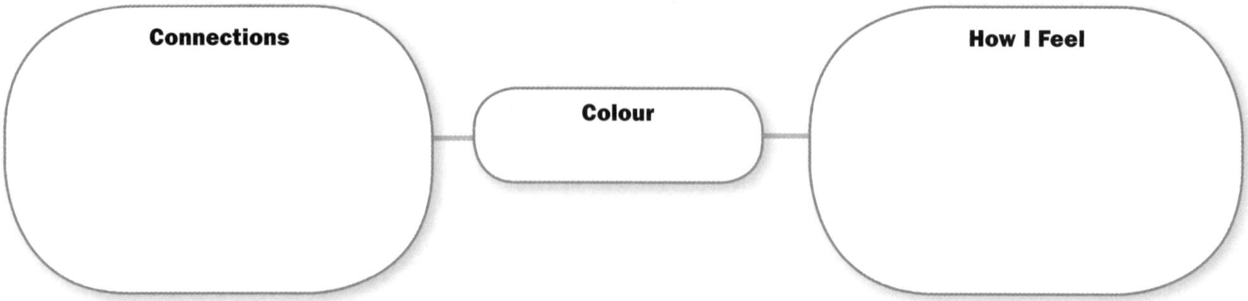

2. Plan your writing. You'll need to begin with a topic sentence. It should state your main idea, why you are writing and what you want to say. Write your topic sentence here.

   ____

   Then, you will write a few sentences about your connection to the colour. Finally, you will write a sentence or two about how the colour makes you feel.

2 Write.

1. Go to page 21 in your book. Re-read the model and writing prompt.
2. Write your first draft. Check for organisation, content, punctuation, capitalisation and spelling.
3. Check your final draft. Share it with your teacher and classmates.

Now I can ...

· talk about colours and why they are important.

Give an example of a colour and what people usually associate it with.

☐ Yes, I can!
☐ I think I can.
☐ I need more practice.

____

Write a sentence that describes how colour can make you feel.

____

____

· use comparatives and superlatives to compare two or more things.

Write a sentence with a comparative about two colours or things.

☐ Yes, I can!
☐ I think I can.
☐ I need more practice.

____

Write a sentence with a superlative about how one colour or thing is *the most, the best,* and so on.

____

· use *the* to identify general and specific things.

☐ Yes, I can!
☐ I think I can.
☐ I need more practice.

Fill in the blanks with *the* and *a/an*.

Sara bought _____ interesting painting. My favourite part of _____ painting is _____ sun.

The artist used _____ colour orange instead of yellow. It creates _____ happy feeling.

· write a paragraph about my favourite colour.

☐ Yes, I can!
☐ I think I can.
☐ I need more practice.

Write a topic sentence about another colour you like. The topic sentence should include why you are writing and what you want to say.

____

____

____

YOU DECIDE **Choose an activity.** Go to page 90.

Unit 2

Feeling Good?

1 **Unscramble the words.** Then write the letters in the circles to answer the question below.

ISRVSEU	(___) ___ ___ ___ ___ ___ ___
DAINVE	___ ___ ___ (___) ___ ___
ABATERIC	___ ___ (___) ___ ___ ___ ___ ___
LECL	(___) ___ ___ ___
MIENMU MESTYS	(___) ___ ___ ___ ___ ___ ___ ___ ___ ___ ___ ___
SINNOFECTI	___ (___) ___ ___ ___ ___ ___ ___ ___ ___
RATET	___ ___ ___ (___) ___
TPOTECR	___ ___ ___ ___ ___ ___ (___)
GISETD	___ (___) ___ ___ ___ ___
ROES	___ (___) ___ ___
TOCANITIBIS	___ (___) ___ ___ ___ ___ ___ ___ ___ ___ ___
MYPSTSOM	___ ___ ___ ___ ___ ___ ___ (___)

How can you protect yourself from viruses?

___ ___ ___ ___ ___ ___ ___ ___ ___ ___ ___ ___

2 **Match the word to its definition.** Write the letter on the line.

____ 1. bacteria	a. medicine that treats illnesses
____ 2. viruses	b. one-cell organisms that can be good for the body
____ 3. antibiotic	c. the body's defence against illness
____ 4. immune system	d. signs of illness
____ 5. symptoms	e. tiny organisms that need a host to survive

3 **Fill in the blanks.** Complete each sentence with a word from the box.

antibiotics	bacteria	digest	disease	emotions
positive	survive	vaccinations	viruses	

1. When people feel ill and weak, they may be fighting a ________________.
2. Illnesses are caused by ________________ and ________________.
3. One way to protect against viruses is to get ________________.
4. Viruses cannot be treated with ________________.
5. Bacteria are cells that can ________________ inside and outside of the body.
6. Bacteria help us ________________ food and feel our ________________.
7. It's important to stay ________________ when we are ill.

4 **Listen.** Circle the vocabulary word you hear being described. 007

vaccinations	sore	symptoms
cells	invade	emotions
viruses	protect	bacteria
immune system	infections	illnesses
antibiotics	treat	positive

5 **Listen.** Answer each question. You may look at the words from the lists above to help you. 008

1. *Some symptoms of a cold are a sore throat and sneezing.*
2. ________________
3. ________________
4. ________________

GRAMMAR

Adverbs: Saying how and how often you do something

Max **often** goes to bed after midnight.	**Often**, Max goes to bed after midnight.
He is **always** tired.	
Kara **sometimes** wakes up before 7.00.	**Sometimes**, Kara wakes up before 7.00.
She sleeps **well**.	
Caroline **occasionally** goes to bed by 9.00.	**Occasionally**, Caroline goes to bed by 9.00.
She **always** likes to be rested because she handles problems **better**.	

Some adverbs answer the question '*How often?*' They usually go in front of the verb. (*He always sleeps late.*) Note that these adverbs follow the verb *to be*. (*He is always at home.*) Some adverbs answer the question *How?* They usually go after the verb. (*She sleeps well.*)

1 **Listen.** Write the adverb you hear. Then tick whether it describes '*How?*' or '*How often?*' You will hear each sentence twice. 009

Adverb	How	How Often
well	✓	

2 **Complete the sentences.** Put the adverbs in the correct place.

1. If we __________________ sleep __________________ , we'll stay healthier. (enough)
2. __________________ , most/Most mammals need __________________ a good night's sleep. (usually)
3. Some people __________________ get __________________ a good night's sleep. (rarely)
4. __________________ , some/Some people fall asleep more __________________ than others. (easily)
5. When we __________________ sleep __________________ , we can get ill. (poorly)
6. When we __________________ sleep __________________ , we can think clearly. (well)
7. Humans sleep in beds, but chimpanzees __________________ sleep __________________ in trees. (usually)
8. Chimpanzees __________________ select __________________ trees that look comfortable. (carefully)

3 **Put the words in the correct order to form sentences.**

1. positively / we / think / sleep / we / well / when

____

2. ill / enough / we / don't / when / sleep / get / we / can / easily / more

____

3. than / I / hours / sleep / more / for / rarely / seven

____

4. for / sleep / I / sometimes / hours / ten

____

1 **Listen and read.** As you read, think about the main idea of each paragraph. 010

The Benefits of Playing Video Games

[1] Imagine that somebody told you to play more video games. Would you wonder why? Well, believe it or not, video games can be good for you. Can you believe it? We often hear that video games are bad for you. But research now shows that video games can positively affect the adolescent brain.

[2] Studies show that when you play video games, your brain works faster. You also pay more attention and remember things better. These games can also help you make decisions and solve problems more quickly and easily.

[3] Another benefit of video games is that it can improve eyesight. Studies show that people who don't normally play video games improve their eyesight after a period of time playing them. In fact, doctors use video games to treat vision problems. For example, some people have one healthy eye and another that is not as strong. To strengthen the weak eye, people play video games and cover up the stronger eye.

[4] Video games can even lower stress and help adolescents with their emotions. Researchers say that video games with different social scenes provide young people with real-world emotional experiences. For example, players can feel excited about doing well or feel disappointed if things don't go their way. Players get to practise their emotions, so they are more prepared to handle them in the real world.

[5] Finally, video games can prepare adolescents for jobs. For example, young people who play video games often have strong technology skills. These skills will be more and more important as our world continues to become more and more technical and digitised.

2 **Read.** Then tick **T** for *True* or **F** for *False*. Re-write the false statements to make them true.

	T	F
1. We often hear about the bad effects of video games.	☐	☐
2. Video games can treat infections.	☐	☐
3. Players don't experience real-world emotions when they play video games.	☐	☐
4. Video games can help you make decisions quickly.	☐	☐

____

____

3 **Read 'The Benefits of Playing Video Games' again.** Fill in the table with the main idea of each paragraph.

Paragraph	Main Idea
1	*Video games can have positive effects.*
2	
3	
4	
5	

4 **Write.** You have read about how the activities you do can affect your brain and overall health. Keep your readings in mind and answer these questions.

1. Apart from playing video games, name an activity that you spend a lot of time doing.

____

2. What skills do you use for this activity?

____

____

3. How might this activity help you in the future?

____

GRAMMAR

***Make* + adjective: Saying what affects mood and feelings**

Subject	*Make*	Object	(feel)	Adjective
Some viruses	make	you	feel	ill.
A positive experience	makes	you	feel	happy.
Video games	can make	a person	feel	relaxed.
Exams	make	some students	feel	stressed.

We use *make* + adjective to describe how a person feels as a result of something. The subject is the cause or the reason why a person feels a certain way.

1 **Complete the sentences.** Use the correct form of *make*.

1. Eating well ______________ me healthy.
2. Viruses ______________ people ill.
3. Antibiotics can ______________ you feel better.
4. It ______________ me nervous when I get a vaccination.
5. Video games ______________ people focused.
6. Taking a test can ______________ you nervous.

2 **Listen.** Complete the answer to each question. Use *make* or *makes* + an adjective from the word bank. 011

depressed	**excited**	**happy**	**hungry**	**nervous**	**sad**	**sleepy**	**stressed**

1. They ______________________________.
2. It can ______________________________.
3. The doctor ______________________________.
4. Feeling ill ______________________________.
5. Video games ______________________________.

3 **Read Rob's letter that asks for school to start later.** Then write four sentences about how his plan will affect your mood or feelings. Use *make* or *makes* + an adjective in each sentence.

Dear School Board,

As the teachers and staff know, most students have trouble paying attention in the mornings. That is because we are young teens and need as much sleep as we can get. We cannot focus because not getting enough sleep makes us tired. I know this from personal experience. Also, I have read several studies that show that the adolescent brain needs a lot of rest.

I have a plan that I hope will make everyone happy. I think that school should start 30 minutes later. That way, students can sleep a little longer. This will make us more focused in the mornings. More sleep will also help us control our emotions. For example, it will help us respond to challenges more positively. More sleep can even make our immune systems stronger!

Will this make school end later? No. My plan suggests that we shorten each class by a few minutes. That will give us 15 more minutes. Also, we will end lunch 15 minutes early. School can then end at the same time.

I hope you will consider my plan. It would make me happy. I want to help my fellow students! Thank you for your time.

Sincerely,

Rob Martin

Sleeping later will make me feel rested.

____

____

____

____

WRITING

When you write a classification essay, you classify, or sort, your topic into categories. For example, if your topic is the 'negative effects of stress', each negative effect will be a category. Once you decide on the categories, present each one and support it with examples. Use the following phrases to help you organise your essay:

- additionally
- another
- another type / way
- to begin with
- the final type / way
- finally
- first
- one type / way

1 Organise.

1. Your topic is *The Negative Effects of Stress*. Re-read the essay on page 37 of your book. Think about the negative effects of stress. What are they? These will be your categories. List four here.

Categories: Negative Effects of Stress	
______________________	______________________
______________________	______________________

2. Organise your writing. Circle the phrase you want to use and write the effect (from above) and an example on the lines below:

Phrases	Category / Effect	Example
1. to begin with / first	______________	______________
2. additionally / one way	______________	______________
3. another way / additionally	______________	______________
4. finally / the final way	______________	______________

2 Write.

1. Go to page 37 in your book. Re-read the model and writing prompt.
2. Write your first draft. Check for organisation, content, punctuation, capitalisation and spelling.
3. Write your final draft. Share it with your teacher and classmates.

Now I can ...

· talk about things that affect my body and mind.

☐ Yes, I can!
☐ I think I can.
☐ I need more practice.

How can sleep affect your health?

____

How can stress affect your emotions?

____

· use adverbs to talk about how and how often I do something.

☐ Yes, I can!
☐ I think I can.
☐ I need more practice.

Put the adverbs in the correct place.

1. When people ______________ sleep ______________, they ______________ don't become ______________ stressed. (enough / easily)
2. People who ______________ sleep ______________, react to ______________ challenges ______________.(well / positively)

· use *make* + adjective to talk about how I feel.

☐ Yes, I can!
☐ I think I can.
☐ I need more practice.

Use *make* + adjective to answer the questions.

How do you feel when you have a virus?

____

How do you feel before you take a test?

____

· write a classification essay about the negative effects of stress.

☐ Yes, I can!
☐ I think I can.
☐ I need more practice.

Write three sentences of how stress affects you negatively. Use three phrases you learnt to organise your writing.

____

____

____

YOU DECIDE **Choose an activity.** Go to page 91.

Units 1–2 Review

1 **Read.** Choose the correct answer.

1. Blue is a ____ colour.
   a. most common   b. common   c. more common than

2. The colour green makes people ____ the colour red.
   a. more relaxed than   b. the most relaxed   c. relaxed

3. Red flashing lights usually make people ____ than yellow lights.
   a. the most nervous   b. more nervous   c. nervous

4. Yellow is one of ____ colours.
   a. bright   b. more brighter than   c. the brightest

5. Ari likes purple ____ blue.
   a. best   b. better than   c. better

6. Purple was once a ____ colour.
   a. more luxurious   b. the most luxurious   c. luxurious

2 **Read about the first colour photograph.** Decide which answer (a, b or c) best fits each gap.

Did you know that photographs weren't always in colour? They were in black and white, or in (1) ____ brownish colour. (2) ____ scientist in Scotland took (3) ____ first colour photo in 1861. (4) ____ scientist's name was James Clerk Maxwell. (5) ____ photo he took was of (6) ____ colourful ribbon tied in a bow. To make the colour photo, he took three different photos. (7) ____ first photo was with a red filter. (8) ____ filter is like a window with colour he put over the camera's lens. (9) ____ next photo was in blue. And (10) ____ last photo was in yellow. When Maxwell put (11) ____ three photos together, he created (12) ____ very first colour photograph!

	a	b	c		a	b	c
1.	a. the	b. a	c. an	**7.**	a. The	b. A	c. An
2.	a. The	b. A	c. An	**8.**	a. The	b. A	c. An
3.	a. the	b. a	c. an	**9.**	a. The	b. A	c. An
4.	a. The	b. A	c. An	**10.**	a. the	b. a	c. an
5.	a. The	b. A	c. An	**11.**	a. the	b. a	c. an
6.	a. the	b. a	c. an	**12.**	a. the	b. a	c. an

3 **Write.** Use the words to write one or two sentences.

1. enough / sleep / tired When I do not sleep enough, I am tired.
2. often / ill / immune system / strong ______
3. always / antibiotics / regularly ______
4. usually / vaccinations / protect / viruses ______
5. sometimes / wake up / easily ______
6. occasionally / rest / quietly / my room ______
7. sleep / well / negative / experiences ______
8. always / better / bed / early ______

4 **Write.** Change the sentences so that the meaning is the same. Use *make* or *makes*.

1. I feel ill when I eat onions.
   Onions make me (feel) ill.
2. I am happy when I have positive experiences.
   ______
3. Some students feel stressed when they have exams.
   ______
4. Most people feel ill when they have a virus.
   ______
5. I feel nervous when I get a vaccination.
   ______
6. Some people are relaxed when they play video games.
   ______
7. When I study maths, I feel focused.
   ______

Unit 3

Your Virtual Self

1 **Follow the steps.** Then fill in the words that are left to show the secret message.

machine	information	communicate
access	tools	instant
improve	constant	digital
technology	ability	location

1. Cross out the words that begin with 'i'.
2. Cross out the word that means 'to share information'.
3. Cross out the word that means 'place'.
4. Cross out the word that means 'the power or skill to do something'.
5. Cross out the word that completes this sentence: ______ extend our physical abilities.
6. Cross out the word that completes this sentence: A car is an example of a ______ that we use to make our lives easier.

Secret Message:

____________ ____________ gives people

____________ ____________ to one another.

2 **Match the word or phrase to its definition.** Write the letter on the line.

_____	1. to take over	a. without stopping
_____	2. to improve	b. to take control of
_____	3. instant	c. a way of reaching someone or entering a place
_____	4. constant	d. to make better
_____	5. access	e. happening very quickly

3 **Listen.** Circle **T** for *True* or **F** for *False.* 012

1.	T	F	4.	T	F
2.	T	F	5.	T	F
3.	T	F	6.	T	F

4 **Listen again.** Correct the false statements. 013

____

____

____

____

____

____

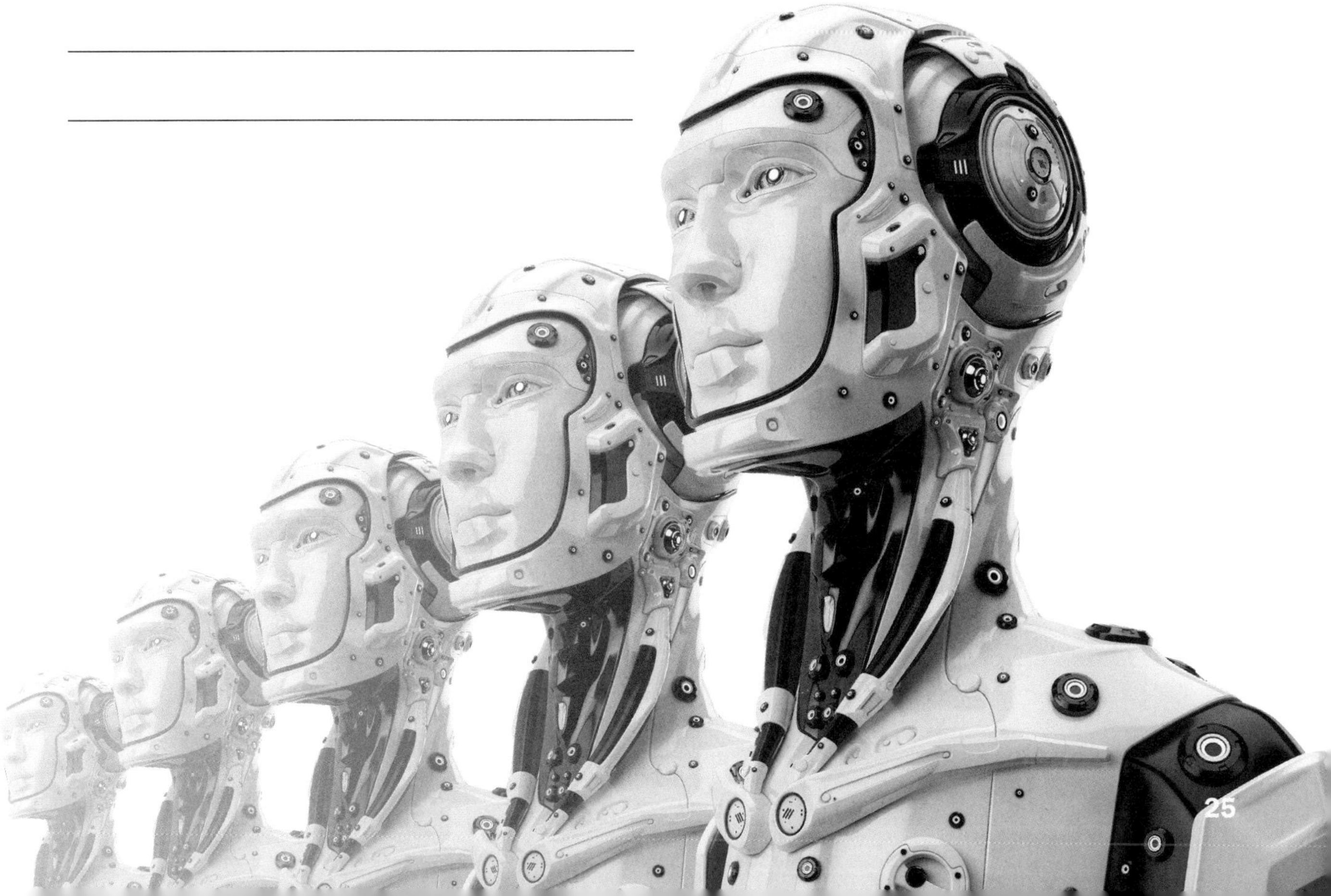

GRAMMAR

Modals: Expressing obligation, advice and permission

Obligation Students **have to/must** turn off their phones during tests. They don't have to turn off their phones between lessons.
Advice Students **should** put away their mobile phones in class. They **shouldn't** let their phones interfere with their studies.
Permission **Can** students use their computers to go online during lessons? They **can/may** if it is for that lesson. They **can't/may not** go online to access social media.

Have to and *must* show obligation, while *don't have to* shows there is no obligation. *Should/shouldn't* show advice. *Can* and *may* show permission, while *can't* and *may not* show there is no permission. Note that we use *can/can't* a lot more often than we use *may/may not*.

1 **Read.** Circle the word that completes each sentence.

On social media, we (1) **should** / **can** connect and communicate with others. And we (2) **may** / **have to** find people with similar interests. We (3) **must** / **can** share ideas with our new friends even if we aren't in the same location. Even though we don't see our new friends face to face, they (4) **must** / **can** become important people in our lives. This is why social media (5) **can** / **should** be so amazing. We all (6) **should** / **have to** be thankful to technology for bringing people together. With social media, it (7) **can't** / **shouldn't** be hard for anyone to be connected.

2 **Write.** Write three sentences using the means of expression in brackets.

1. (show obligation) ____

____

2. (give advice) ____

____

3. (give permission) ____

____

3 **Listen.** Write your answers using *have to, must, should, can* or *may*. You can also use the negative forms. 014

1. *You should create a safe password.*
2. ______
3. ______
4. ______
5. ______
6. ______
7. ______

4 **Write.** Think of rules and advice for using media in the classroom. Use at least one word from the box and *have to, must, should, can* or *may* for each rule. You can also use the negative forms.

access	**communicate**	**digital**	**information**	**interfere**
Internet	**private**	**share**	**social media**	**technology**

1. *We can be on social media until class starts.*
2. ______
3. ______
4. ______
5. ______
6. ______

1 Listen and read. As you read, think about tasks you want, or don't want, robots to do in your home. 015

Robots Working in Your Home?

Cyborg anthropologist Amber Case says that today, most people are like cyborgs. She says that although we are human, we are also part machine. We're part machine because we rely on technology so much. So, if we are cyborgs, what is a machine that has human abilities and features? A robot?

Robots, or robotic machines, build and assemble things in factories. They are digitally programmed to do specific jobs, like put together the parts of a car. These robots do the same task over and over again. They can do jobs that humans used to do, but they are not like humans at all. They are just very fancy tools.

However, scientists are making new kinds of robots. These robots are programmed to act like humans. Some even look like humans. They can communicate with us and do many different tasks. The purpose of some of these robots is to take over human jobs in our homes, schools and at work. For example, there are robots that can babysit, take care of old people, and take and deliver food orders. Someday, robots may even be able to cook our meals and fold our laundry!

These robots do not fit the definition of the 'calm technology' Amber talks about. Instead of working quietly in the background, these human-like robots will constantly be around us. Will the jobs these robots do improve our lives? Will their constant interruptions to our private lives be worth it? We may have to try living with one before we know for sure.

2 **Read each statement.** Then tick **T** for *True* or **F** for *False*. Re-write the false statements to make them true.

	T	F
1. Robots are part human and part machine.	☐	☐
2. Robots have the ability to take care of people.	☐	☐
3. Someday, we will be able to communicate with robots.	☐	☐
4. Human-like robots are a kind of 'calm technology'.	☐	☐

____

____

3 **Read 'Robots Working in Your Home?' again.** Write a list of tasks and activities that you or others do in your home. Then tick whether you would like a robot or a human to do that task or activity.

Task or Activity	Robot	Human
Play games with me		✔

4 **Write.** You have read about calm technology and robots working in your home. Which would you like to have? Why?

____

____

____

____

____

GRAMMAR

***Must*, *might* and *can't*: Expressing certainty**

He **can't** email you tonight. He hasn't got access to the Internet.	very certain, impossible
There **must** be two people with the same username. That's not the same person I saw on social media yesterday.	very certain, sure
The information on that website **might** be wrong. I don't believe that horses have got two stomachs.	mostly certain, possible

We use *must*, *might* and *can't* to express how sure we are that something is true. Use *can't* when something is impossible. Use *must* when you are certain that something is true. Finally, use *might* when you are mostly certain about something. *Might* doesn't show as much certainty as *must* and *can't*. Note that we don't usually use *can* or *mustn't* to express certainty.

1 **Read.** Circle the word that best completes each sentence.

1. Juan **might** / **must** have an unusual username. He never remembers it.
2. Amelia loves her cat so much. Her password **might** / **can't** be her cat's name.
3. I read on three websites that horses have got one stomach. It **must** / **can't** be true.
4. Her little brother **might** / **can't** be the same age as my sister. Her brother is in Year 7 and my sister is in Year 10.
5. Some robots **might** / **must** have the ability to play football. Check a few sources to find out.

2 **Listen.** Some statements are true and some are false. Use *must*, *might* and *can't* to write what you believe. 016

1. That can't be true. The average mobile phone can last a few hours without recharging it.
2. ______
3. ______
4. ______
5. ______

3 **Read Helen's blog.** Write two responses. Use *must, might* and *can't* to write what you do and don't believe.

Helen's Travel & Adventure Blog

Hello Friends! Today I want to tell you about my dad's trip to New Zealand. He went for work. It took him three days to get there. He said he didn't sleep at all on the plane. But that can't be true. My dad falls asleep reading while on his computer all the time. He even fell asleep at the dinner table once! My dad must be the sleepiest person in the world.

On his day off, my dad went on an adventure. He floated down a river flowing through a cave. There were even waterfalls as tall as buildings in the cave! Can you believe that? I didn't at first, but it must be true. My dad always tells the truth.

But that's not all. There were twinkling lights all over the cave. Dad said they looked like stars. But guess what? They were worms! Glow worms! He said that New Zealand might be the only place in the world with glow worms like the ones he saw.

Check back next week. A special guest is going to write about one of our national parks!

Kenji

The journey can't take that long. It only takes about 20 hours to get to New Zealand.

Mari

Sounds like a great trip. By the way, my big brother might be sleepier than your dad!

WRITING

In an opinion essay, we want to tell others what we believe about a topic. We express our opinions, and then support those opinions with facts. We find facts in books and on the Internet. We must make it clear when we're stating a fact and when we're expressing an opinion.

When we express an opinion, we say things like:

- I believe ...
- I think ...
- It seems like ...

When stating a fact, we say things like:

- In fact ...
- For example, ...
- Research shows ...

1 Organise.

1. Your topic is *Can we live without our smartphones?* Look through the unit in your book to find facts that support your overall opinion about our use of smartphones and technology. Look on the Internet to find more facts. Make a list of facts and your opinion about the topic in the table below.

My Opinion	Facts

2. Plan your writing. You'll need a topic sentence that describes what the topic of your essay is. Write your topic sentence here:

   ____

   Next, you'll need two or three paragraphs for your essay. Write your opinion and support it with facts.

   Finally, you will need a concluding paragraph. It will express your overall opinion, or argument, in different words.

2 Write.

1. Go to page 55 in your book. Re-read the model and writing prompt.
2. Write your first draft. Check for organisation, content, punctuation, capitalisation and spelling.
3. Write your final draft. Share it with your teacher and classmates.

Now I can ...

· talk about how technology affects our lives.

☐ Yes, I can!
☐ I think I can.
☐ I need more practice.

Use words from the box to write two sentences about technology.

access	ability	communicate	constant	digital	information	location	social media

____

____

· use modals to talk about obligation, advice and permission.

☐ Yes, I can!
☐ I think I can.
☐ I need more practice.

Write one sentence in which you give someone permission to do something.

____

Write one sentence in which you give someone advice about how to take time away from technology.

____

· use *must, might* and *can't* to express certainty.

☐ Yes, I can!
☐ I think I can.
☐ I need more practice.

Fill in the blanks with *must, might* or *can't*.

Your dad ______ be a really good cook. You always tell me about the great food he makes.

That gift ______ be from Uncle Mark. He never remembers my birthday.

· write an opinion essay about smartphones.

☐ Yes, I can!
☐ I think I can.
☐ I need more practice.

I think we (can / can't) ______ live without our smartphones because ...

____

____

____

YOU DECIDE **Choose an activity.** Go to page 92.

Unit 4

Underwater Mysteries

1 **Read the sentences.** Then complete the puzzle. You can use your textbook (pages 60–61), for help.

Across

1. I check *Nautilus*'s ______ every day for updates.
2. *Nautilus*'s robots ______ things at the bottom of the sea.
3. Underwater ______ are now easier with technology.
4. Scientists control the robotic ______ .
5. Scientists on *Nautilus* ______ to find shipwrecks.
6. I like to ______ new reports about *Nautilus*.
7. I can check for *Nautilus* updates ______ .
8. To learn more about *Nautilus*, you can send a ______ to the crew.

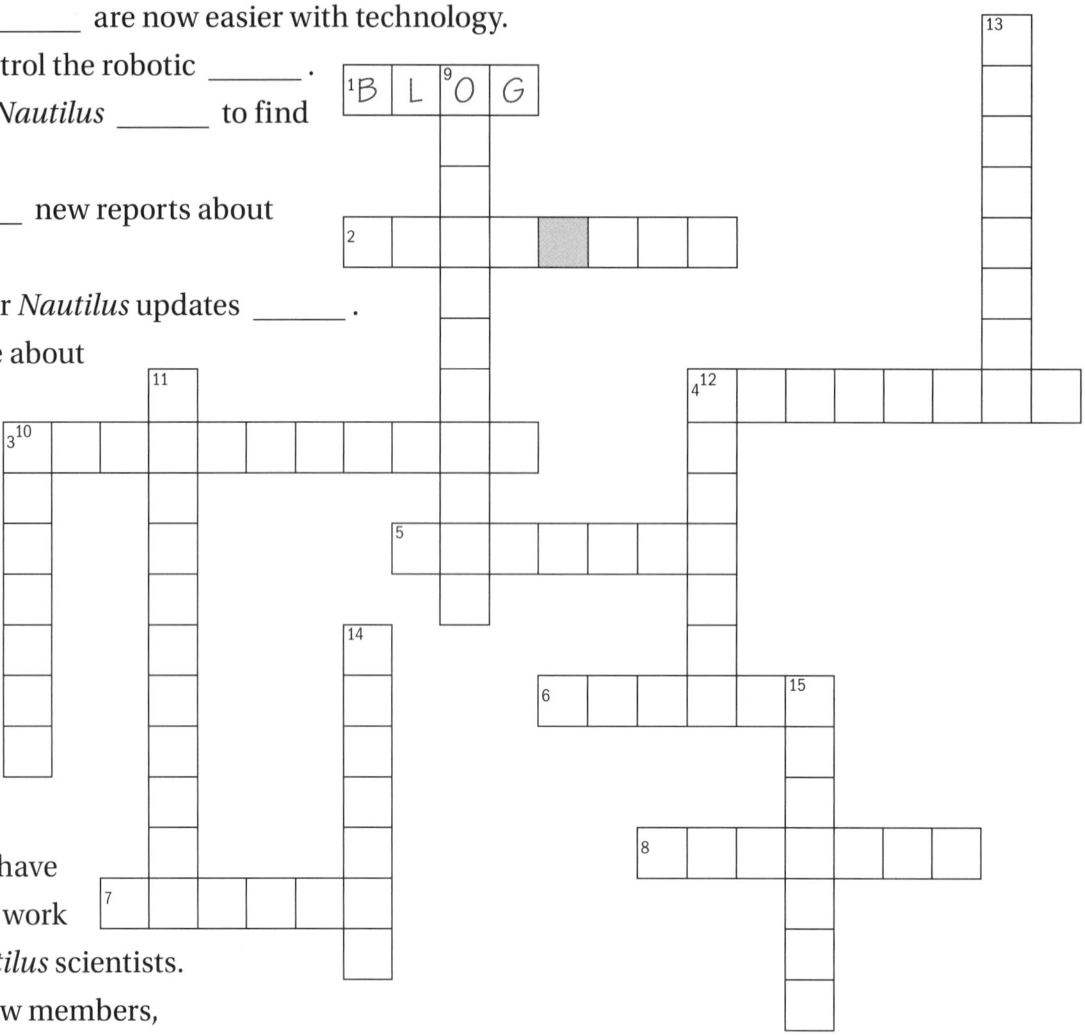

Down

9. Some people have an ______ to work with the *Nautilus* scientists.
10. *Nautilus*'s crew members, like Katy Croff Bell, are underwater ______ .
11. I wonder what *Nautilus*'s next ______ will be?
12. People can be ______ travellers on *Nautilus*.
13. *Nautilus*'s crew communicates with others to make sure their information is ______ .
14. It would be exciting to go on an underwater ______ .
15. For more information, you can look on *Nautilus*'s ______ .

2 **Listen.** Circle **T** for *True* or **F** for *False*. 017

1.	T	F	4.	T	F
2.	T	F	5.	T	F
3.	T	F	6.	T	F

3 **Listen again.** Correct the false statements. 018

____

____

____

4 **Fill in the blanks.** Use the correct form of the words from the box.

attempt	expeditions	expert	find out	look for	make sure	online	opportunity	website

I wanted to learn more about underwater exploration. I (1) ______________________ information (2) ______________________ and found an interesting (3) ______________________. I (4) ______________________ that the first underwater (5) ______________________ were limited by how long the explorer could hold his breath. Explorers wanted the (6) ______________________ to spend more time underwater. As early as the 1700s, explorers (7) ______________________ to build underwater suits. They had to (8) ______________________ that they could breathe underwater. In 1943, Jacques Cousteau, perhaps the most famous underwater (9) ______________________, built a diving suit called an Aqua-Lung. It was very similar to the diving suits we use today.

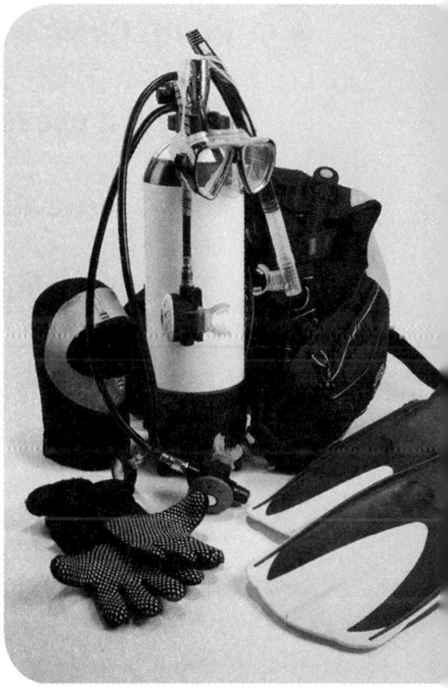

5 **Write.** Imagine you are going on an underwater expedition. Write three sentences using at least one of the words from the box in each sentence.

blog	destination	expert	follow	journey	messages	preparation	transmit	virtual

____

____

____

GRAMMAR

***Used to* and *would*: Talking about habits in the past**

Did you **use to** watch programmes about the sea as a child?

No, I never **used to** watch those programmes.

I **didn't use to** watch television at all.

Years later, when my cousin **used to** go scuba-diving, I became interested in the sea.

Where **did** she **use to** go scuba-diving?

She **used to** / **would** go diving at the beach by the school.

Both *used to* and *would* are used to talk about habits in the past. If the sentence has *did*, use *use to*. Otherwise, use *used to* or *would*.

However, *used to* is only possible with verbs like *be*, *live* and *have*.

1 **Read.** Circle the correct form.

1. Did it **use to** / **used to** take a long time to get ready for an underwater expedition?
2. The crew **used to** / **use to** start each day with a list of things to do.
3. Each explorer **use to** / **used to** be responsible for certain items on the list.
4. The first thing they **use to** / **would** do was to check that everything was in place.
5. If they were missing something, they **would** / **use to** quickly look for what they needed.
6. When did they **use to** /**used to** get together and wish each other luck?

2 **Complete the sentences.** Use *used to*, *would* or *use to.*

1. Did you ______________ read books about the sea?
2. Meag ______________ read dozens of books about the sea.
3. Every week, she ______________ go to the library to look for books.
4. All the books ______________ be about ocean wildlife and underwater exploration.
5. She didn't ______________ look for books about anything else.
6. She ______________ come home with at least ten books.
7. Each night, Meag ______________ look at the pictures and read her books before bed.
8. In the morning, she ______________ tell her dad all about everything she learnt.

3 **Listen.** Re-write the sentences you hear with *used to* or *didn't use to.* 019

1. Before aeroplanes, people didn't use to travel across the Atlantic too often.
2. ______________
3. ______________
4. ______________
5. ______________
6. ______________
7. ______________

4 **Write.** Think about what travel by ship, train or on horseback used to be like. Write four new sentences with *used to* or *would.*

____

____

____

____

1 **Listen and read.** As you read, think about the author's purpose. 020

Under Cuban Waters: An Ancient City or a Natural Formation?

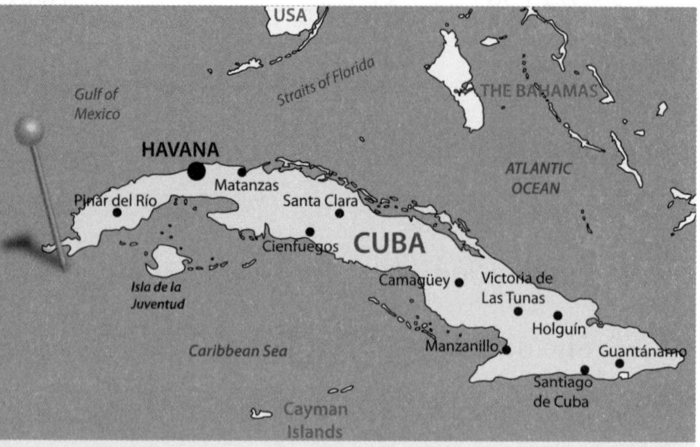

In 2001, underwater explorers found something interesting. Off the western coast of Cuba, they discovered huge stone structures on the ocean floor. At first, they thought the structures were man-made carvings. Was it an ancient city from thousands of years ago? They weren't sure.

The explorers wanted to examine the structures more carefully. They sent a robot 600 metres (2,000 feet) down to take pictures and film the site.

They found out that the site included smooth blocks with right angles, pyramid shapes, and some circular shapes. Some experts believe that the formations are more than 6,000 years old. That's older than the pyramids in Egypt! Paulina Zelitsky is the main explorer who found the structures. She says, 'It's a really wonderful structure which really looks like it could have been a large urban centre.'

Other researchers, however, aren't so sure. Some say the structures are too deep. They ask, 'How did they get there?' They suggest that, over centuries, nature carved the shapes. Cuban marine geologist Manuel Iturralde says that nature can create some really wonderful formations.

Manuel has studied many underwater structures and formations in his career. Still, he cannot accurately identify the formations as natural. He agrees that they are very unusual, and he would have difficulty explaining how they formed naturally.

So, what are these structures under Cuban waters? Are they the remains of an ancient city? Or, are they natural formations? We may never know for sure.

2 **Read.** Then tick **T** for *True* or **F** for *False*. Re-write the false statements to make them true.

	T	F
1. Manuel believes that the site contains the remains of a city.	☐	☐
2. A special robot took photos and filmed the site.	☐	☐
3. Some experts believe the formations are 5,000 years old.	☐	☐
4. We are not sure whether the site is natural or man-made.	☐	☐

____

____

____

3 **Read 'Under Cuban Waters' again.** What are the two main points the author discusses? What is the author's purpose? Fill in the diagram below.

Point 1	Point 2
Author's purpose:	

4 **Write.** There are many similarities between the Cuban site and Yonaguni Jima site that you read about in your book. What are the differences? If you could explore either site, which would you choose? Why?

____

____

____

____

____

____

GRAMMAR

Past simple: Describing past actions

People **built** the Transcontinental Railroad **more than one hundred years ago**. It **was** a big job!

Didn't Mel **start** a blog about underwater explorers **last spring**?

In 1987, scientists **examined** large rock formations under the sea near Yonaguni, Japan.

Did you **run** in that race **a week ago**? My brother and I **planned** to, but we **didn't run**.

We use the past simple to talk about actions or situations that started and finished in the past.

We often use phrases that show the past: *in 1987, a week ago, last spring*.

1 Listen. Change the verbs you hear to the past. 021

1. looked for
2. ______
3. ______
4. ______
5. ______
6. ______
7. ______
8. ______
9. ______
10. ______

2 Write sentences about the past using the phrases and verbs.

1. (more than 20 years ago, marry) My parents married more than 20 years ago.
2. (last week, study) ______
3. (two years ago, be) ______
4. (in August, find) ______
5. (in 2015, follow) ______
6. (last summer, visit) ______
7. (in April, examine) ______
8. (a month ago, start) ______

3 **Read Marissa's blog.** Write back to her and tell her about a time you saw or found something new or interesting.

Hi, friends! Today I want to tell you about my visit to Puerto Rico. Last summer, I visited my cousin Luis there. Luis took me swimming every day. One day, he showed me something special. He made sure we each had a pair of swimming goggles. We swam just a few metres from the shore. Below us were a lot of rocks. I followed him as he dived under the water. When I opened my eyes, Luis pointed to some strange things all over the rocks. They were spiky and purple! I didn't know what they were. Then I found out that they were sea urchins! Luis helped me carefully pick one up. It didn't hurt me. It was so cool to examine. I had never seen anything like a sea urchin before! Luis told me that people eat their eggs, but we decided to leave them in the sea. I was very happy that Luis showed them to me.

Now, I want to hear from you! Did you recently find or discover something new? When was it? What happened? Thanks!

WRITING

We use special words and phrases to show the differences, or contrasting ideas, about a topic. These words and phrases usually go at the beginning of a sentence.

People believe in mythical creatures. ***At the same time****, nobody can prove that they exist.*

Even though *some people say they saw the Loch Ness Monster, others say it's only a myth.*

- although
- but
- however
- on the other hand
- at the same time
- even though
- instead

1 Organise.

1. Your task is to write about *a mythical creature from your country.* You will need to present different, or contrasting, points of view about the creature. Write down some beliefs about the creature in Column 1. Then write different, or contrasting, beliefs in Column 2.

Column 1	Column 2

2. Now choose which words or phrases you plan to use to show the different, or contrasting, beliefs or points of view. Circle the ones you want to use at the top of the page.

2 Write.

1. Go to page 71 in your book. Re-read the model and writing prompt.
2. Write your first draft. Check for organisation, content, punctuation, capitalisation and spelling.
3. Write your final draft. Share it with your teacher and classmates.

Now I can ...

- ☐ Yes, I can!
- ☐ I think I can.
- ☐ I need more practice.

· talk about underwater exploration.

What kinds of things do underwater explorers find?

____

____

How has underwater exploration changed with recent technology?

____

____

· use *used to* and *would* to talk about habits in the past.

- ☐ Yes, I can!
- ☐ I think I can.
- ☐ I need more practice.

Write two things that scientists used to do when exploring oceans in the past.

____

____

· use the past simple to describe past actions.

- ☐ Yes, I can!
- ☐ I think I can.
- ☐ I need more practice.

Write a statement, a question and a negative statement using the past simple. In each sentence, use a phrase that shows the past.

____

____

____

· write a contrast essay about a mythical creature.

- ☐ Yes, I can!
- ☐ I think I can.
- ☐ I need more practice.

Choose a mythical creature different from the one you wrote about in your essay. Write a belief about it. Then write a contrasting sentence.

____

____

____

YOU DECIDE Choose an activity. Go to page 93.

Units 3–4 Review

1 **Read the list of rules for the library.** Choose the correct answer.

1. Guests ____ turn off the sound on their mobile phones while in the library.
   a. may b. shouldn't c. must
2. If guests need to talk on the phone, they ____ go outside so they do not interrupt others.
   a. should b. don't have to c. may
3. These are not private computers. Anybody ____ use them.
   a. must b. may c. should
4. Each user ____ spend more than 30 minutes at a time on the computers.
   a. doesn't have to b. shouldn't c. can
5. When you have finished using the computer, you ____ log out.
   a. must b. can c. may
6. Guests ____ also access the Internet on their own devices with a password from the librarian.
   a. should b. must c. can
7. There is a digital copy machine that guests ____ use on the second floor.
   a. must b. may c. should
8. You ____ use the copier to make more than a few copies.
   a. shouldn't b. don't have to c. must
9. For more information about the technology or machines at the library, guests ____ ask at the front desk.
   a. have to b. can't c. may

2 **Listen to the statements.** Some are true and some are false. Use *must, might* and *can't* to write what you believe. 022

That might be true. My friend's dog smells everything.

___

___

___

___

___

3 **Read.** Then choose the best answer to fill in each blank.

I (1) ____ be interested in the *Titanic* when I was younger. The *Titanic* (2) ____ a British passenger ship on a journey across the Atlantic Ocean. It never (3) ____ its destination. It (4) ____ in the North Atlantic in 1912. Its remains are still at the bottom of the sea. The other day, my mum (5) ____ she (6) ____ interested in the *Titanic* as a child, too. She and her brothers (7) ____ go to the library every day after school. She always (8) ____ this opportunity to look for books about the *Titanic*. She (9) ____ to me that when she was my age, most people (10) ____ computers. People (11) ____ go online whenever they wanted to. If people wanted to find out about something, they usually (12) ____ go to the library.

1. a. would	b. used to	c. use to	**7.** a. used	b. use	c. would
2. a. is	b. would be	c. was	**8.** a. took	b. take	c. takes
3. a. reach	b. reaches	c. reached	**9.** a. explained	b. explain	c. explains
4. a. sank	b. sinks	c. sink	**10.** a. had	b. used to have	c. didn't have
5. a. say	b. said	c. says	**11.** a. can't	b. couldn't	c. could
6. a. was	b. is	c. were	**12.** a. had to	b. have	c. has

4 **Re-write the sentences using *used to* or *use to*.**

1. Before technology, were underwater expeditions more dangerous?

____

2. How long did explorers spend on an expedition?

____

3. How did experts examine remains under the water?

____

4. They did not have diving suits like we have today.

____

5. They took a long time to make careful preparations.

____

6. Ships did not always make it to their destinations.

____

Unit 5

Life in the Extreme

1 **Unscramble the words.** Then use the letters in the circles to complete the sentence below.

EIFL	___ ___ ___ (___)
NOXGEY	___ ___ ___ ___ ___ (___)
VLEEL	___ ___ (___) ___ ___
CATPILY	___ ___ ___ (___) ___ ___ ___
ERAVYIT	___ ___ (___) ___ ___ ___ ___
CKAL FO	___ ___ ___ ___ (___) ___
TICONIONSD	___ ___ ___ ___ ___ ___ ___ ___ (___) ___
SALMAMM	(___) ___ ___ ___ ___ ___ ___
DEAPATD	___ ___ ___ ___ ___ (___) ___
HEDALN	___ ___ (___) ___ ___ ___
TEVIHR	(___) ___ ___ ___ ___ ___
AHRSH	___ ___ ___ (___) ___

There are many animals that live in very harsh

___ ___ ___ ___ ___ ___ ___ ___ ___ ___ ___ ___.

2 **Match the word to its definition.** Write the letter on the line.

_____ 1. thrive	a. change, get used to
_____ 2. lack of	b. surroundings
_____ 3. environment	c. do well
_____ 4. typical	d. not enough
_____ 5. adapt	e. usual, normal

3 **Read.** Complete the sentences with words from the box.

adapt	**conditions**	**creatures**	**harsh**	**mammals**
oxygen	**remarkable**	**thrive**	**variety**	

(1) ____________, such as polar bears, are not the only kind of animals that can live in (2) ____________ (3) ____________. There is a (4) ____________ of (5) ____________ that (6) ____________ in extreme environments. For example, the tardigrade is a tiny organism that can survive without much (7) ____________. It even has the (8) ____________ ability to (9) ____________ to life in outer space!

4 **Listen.** Circle **T** for *True* or **F** for *False.* 023

1.	T	F	2.	T	F	3.	T	F
4.	T	F	5.	T	F	6.	T	F

5 **Listen again.** Correct the false statements. 024

____

____

____

6 **Write two sentences about animals that live in extreme environments.** Use at least two words from the box in each sentence.

adapt	**creature**	**conditions**	**exist**	**handle**	**harsh**	**lack of**	**thrive**

1. ____

2. ____

GRAMMAR

Present perfect: Describing past experiences that connect to the present

There are many creatures that **we've never seen** that **have adapted** to extreme environments.
Scientists **have studied** extremophiles for years to learn about the origins of life on Earth.
I've already found several books on extremophiles, but I **haven't read** them yet.
Have you **ever been** in an extreme environment?
The study of extremophiles **has helped** us think about life on other planets. ↑ ***have / has* + past participle**

We use the present perfect to talk about experiences or actions that:

- happened in the past, but continue to have a connection in the present (the result of the experience is still felt in the present);
- began in the past, but are still continuing in the present;
- happened recently, but we don't know or say when exactly they happened.

We also often use the present perfect with expressions of time, such as *ever, never, yet* and *already*. Use *yet* in questions and negative statements when you expect something has happened or will happen soon. Use *already* in positive statements when something happened earlier than expected.

1 **Read.** Complete the sentences with the present perfect forms of the verb in brackets.

1. ______________________ (you / ever / wonder) if life exists in outer space?
2. Kevin Hand ______________________ (think) about life on other planets a lot.
3. He ______________________ (visit) several extreme environments.
4. In places like Alaska, Kevin ______________________ (study) a variety of extremophiles.
5. These remarkable creatures ______________________ (thrive) under harsh conditions.
6. They ______________________ (give) Kevin ideas about how animals might exist on other planets.
7. Kevin ______________________ (not go) to outer space yet, but he hopes to someday.

2 **Listen.** Answer the questions using the present perfect. You may use *never, ever* or *yet* as necessary. 025

1. I have never visited Antarctica.
2. ____________________
3. ____________________
4. ____________________
5. ____________________

3 **Read.** Complete the dialogues using the present perfect. You may use *ever, never, yet* or *already* as necessary.

1. Pablo: ____________________?
   Arturo: Yes, I have already seen the polar bear cubs at the zoo.
2. Mia: Has your uncle been to Antarctica?
   Sergio: Yes, ____________________.
3. Mia: Have you ever wanted to go somewhere that cold?
   Sergio: No, ____________________.
4. Mia: ____________________?
   Sergio: No, my uncle has never visited an extremely hot place.
5. Ender: Have scientists already found life on Jupiter's moon?
   Sara: ____________________.
6. Miguel: Have extremophiles thrived in high-pressure environments?
   Jose: ____________________.
7. Marissa: ____________________?
   Jose: No, the chemicals in the water have never killed any of the microbes.
8. Ender: Have you ever wanted to visit outer space?
   Ana: ____________________.

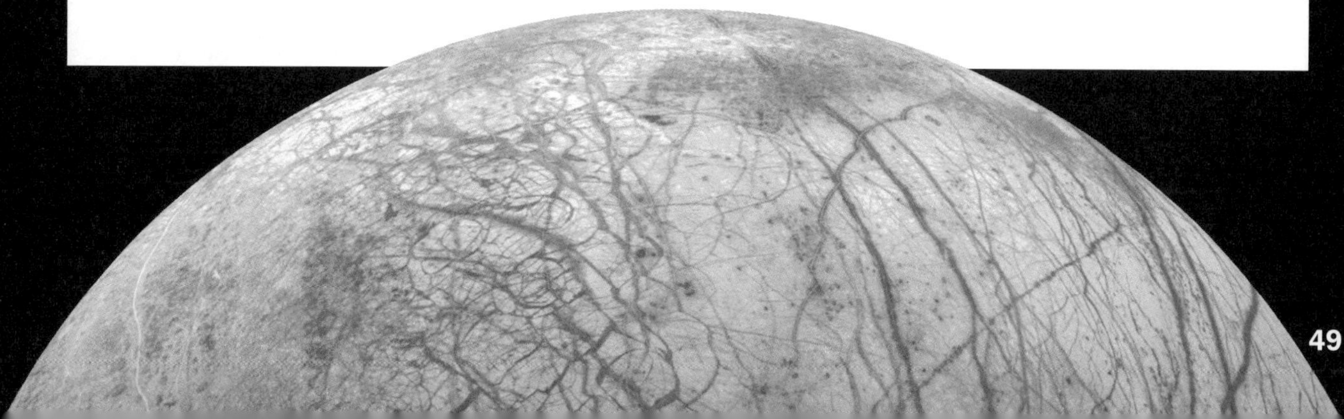

1 **Listen and read.** As you read, notice what type of information is given about each animal.
026

BIZARRE CREATURES

A fruit bat, called the Yoda Bat, has recently been discovered in the rain forest of Papua New Guinea. It is called the Yoda Bat because its big, pointy ears make it look like the *Star Wars* character, Yoda. The Yoda Bat has also got large, yellow eyes and large, open nostrils that add to its bizarre appearance. Since the Yoda Bat is a recent discovery, scientists have not had much time to study it and learn about its diet. They do know, however, that the Yoda Bat eats fruits that grow in the rain forest.

With big, front claws and long tails, scorpions look scary. These very adaptable creatures exist all over the world in deserts and forests. A scorpion's typical meal is made up of insects. But they also eat a variety of other things, including small mammals, reptiles and birds. When scorpions can't find food, they can slow their bodies down and survive on as little as one insect a year. They also have the remarkable ability to use very little oxygen. These abilities help scorpions thrive in some of the planet's harshest environments. The only conditions that scorpions can't handle are environments that lack soil or sand. This is because they burrow, or dig, under the ground.

The anglerfish certainly is ugly. These fish have got big heads and giant mouths full of teeth you can see through. Their most remarkable feature is a rod-like spine that sticks out and hangs over their head. This rod is much like a fishing rod. It gives off a light that attracts small fish for the anglerfish to eat. Anglerfish are normally about 30 cm. (11 in.) long, but can grow up to one m. (3 ft.). They live in the dark, cold depths of the Atlantic and Antarctic Oceans.

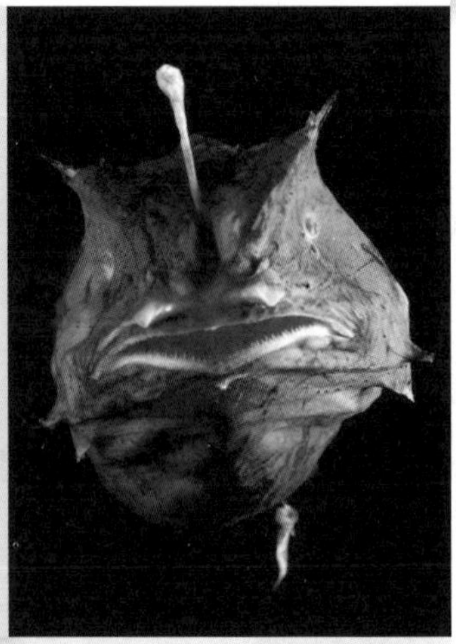

2 **Read each statement.** Then write the name of the animal from the reading that matches each statement.

1. Easily adapts to harsh conditions: ______________________
2. Has got big, pointy ears: ______________________
3. Attracts prey with a rod: ______________________
4. Can survive with little oxygen: ______________________
5. Eats fruits that grow in the rain forest: ______________________

3 **Read 'Bizarre Creatures' again.** Organise information about the animals using the categories below.

Animal	Appearance	Habitat	Diet	Other Details
Yoda Bat	big, pointy ears,			
Scorpion				can slow body down,
Anglerfish				

4 **Read and write.** You have read about six bizarre creatures. Answer the questions about them below.

1. Which of the animals do you think is the ugliest? Why?

____

____

____

2. Which of the animals do you think is the most remarkable? Why?

____

____

____

GRAMMAR

***As . . . as*: Making comparisons of equality**

The anglerfish is just **as remarkable as** the horsehair worm.
Gazelles can't run **as fast as** cheetahs.
Some hummingbirds weigh **as little as** a large spider.
Chimpanzees have got almost **as many** bones in their bodies **as** humans.

We use *as* ... *as* to express how two things are similar or the same.

1 **Read and complete the sentences.** Use expressions of equality.

1. A pygmy shrew is ________________ (small) a hummingbird.
2. The purple pig-nosed frog is just ________________ (ugly) the blobfish.
3. Bizarre creatures are ________________ (important) attractive ones.
4. Many deep-sea fish are ________________ (blind) moles.
5. The axolotl is ________________ (interesting) the tardigrade.
6. Blue whales are ________________ (long) two city buses.
7. Fish need oxygen ________________ (much) humans do.
8. The Sahara Desert is ________________ (harsh) the Antarctic.

2 **Listen.** Re-write the sentences using expressions of equality. 027

1. (Greenland / Siberia) *Greenland's environment is as harsh as Siberia's.*
2. (Lake Vanda / Lake Assal) ________________
3. (baby elephants / two small people) ________________
4. (black-eyed tree frog / Philippine crocodile) ________________
5. (mammals / heat / cold) ________________

3 **Read the webpage.** Then follow the directions below.

The World's Most Wonderful Creatures

We Should Thank Spiders, Not Squash Them
By Stacey Parks

Some people don't think ugly or creepy creatures are as important as cute animals. But these people are wrong. Sometimes creepy animals are even more important than cuddly ones.

For example, many people treat spiders like they don't matter. They step on them and kill them as fast as you can say 'Gotcha!' They don't realise that spiders are an important part of our environment.

Spiders are nature's bug spray. A spider eats about 2,000 insects a year! All spiders, whether as tiny as the end of a pencil or as big as a hand, eat insects. Without spiders, a lot more bugs like cockroaches and mosquitoes would thrive. Cockroaches and mosquitoes can carry disease, so think twice before you smack that spider with a newspaper.

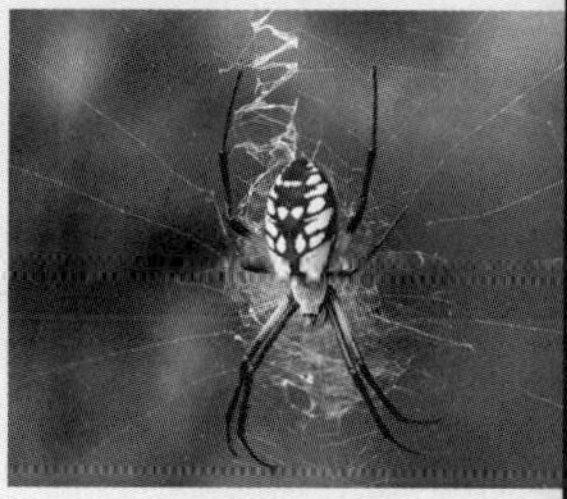

Gardeners and farmers like spiders because spiders eat insects that would otherwise eat the plants and foods they grow.

Spiders are also important because their venom, or poison, has healing powers. Scientists are studying spider venom to see how it can cure certain diseases.

So, the next time you see a spider and want to stamp on it, say 'Thank you' instead!

4 **Write three sentences about animals using expressions of equality and words from the box.**

adaptable	big	bizarre	cute	helpful	important	interesting	remarkable	typical

Spiders are as helpful as bug spray.

____

____

____

WRITING

In persuasive writing we try to get others to agree with our opinion or point of view. We support our point of view with several facts. To connect our ideas, we can use transitional phrases like:

- also
- as a result (of)
- for this reason/these reasons
- another
- because
- therefore

1 Organise.

1. Your task is to write a *persuasive essay about why we should protect an unusual, endangered animal* of your choice. Look on the Internet to find facts about the animal you choose. List facts that support your reasons for wanting to protect this animal.

Animal:	
Reasons	**Facts**

2. Plan your writing. You'll need a topic sentence that expresses your point of view. Write your topic sentence here:

   ____

   Next, you'll need two or three paragraphs for your essay. These will include the facts about the animal you chose.

   Finally, you will need a concluding paragraph. It will restate your point of view in different words and summarise the facts.

2 Write.

1. Go to page 89 in your book. Re-read the model and writing prompt.
2. Write your first draft. Check for organisation, content, punctuation, capitalisation and spelling.
3. Write your final draft. Share it with your teacher and classmates.

Now I can ...

· talk about creatures that live in extreme conditions.

☐ Yes, I can!
☐ I think I can.
☐ I need more practice.

Use words from the box to write two sentences about animals that live in extreme conditions.

adapt	Arctic	conditions	exist	extreme	extremophiles	handle	harsh	thrive

1. ______________________________
2. ______________________________

· use the present perfect to talk about experiences.

☐ Yes, I can!
☐ I think I can.
☐ I need more practice.

Write sentences using the present perfect.

1. wettest / place / be ______________________________
2. weirdest / animal / see ______________________________
3. you / ever / visit / ? ______________________________

· use *as ... as* to make comparisons.

☐ Yes, I can!
☐ I think I can.
☐ I need more practice.

Use expressions of equality to re-write the sentences.

1. Both dolphins and gorillas are extremely intelligent.

____

2. There are 31 days in July. There is the same number in December.

____

· write a persuasive essay about an endangered animal.

☐ Yes, I can!
☐ I think I can.
☐ I need more practice.

Choose one animal you have read about in your book or workbook. Write a topic sentence saying why you think it is remarkable. Support your opinion with a fact.

____

____

____

YOU DECIDE Choose an activity. Go to page 94.

Unit 6

Are You Going to Eat That?

1 **Follow the steps.** Then use the words that are left to complete the secret message.

rotten	nutritious	landfill
challenge	fields	supermarket
appearance	produce	supply
edible	standards	consumers

1. Cross out the word that has two 'd's' in it.
2. Cross out the word that means 'people who buy things'.
3. Cross out the word that means 'provide or give'.
4. Cross out the word that means the opposite of an easy task.
5. Cross out the word that completes this sentence:
   I buy food at the ______________________ .
6. Cross out the word that is the name for a place where rubbish is buried.
7. Cross out the words that complete this sentence:
   Lots of ______________________ food sits in ______________________ and is never taken to the supermarket.

Secret Message:

The ______________________ of fruit and vegetables does not matter.
Ugly ______________________ is ______________________ and
______________________ .

2 **Match each word to its definition.** Write the letter on the line.

_____ 1. waste	a. a series of activities working toward one result
_____ 2. shocking	b. the way something looks
_____ 3. campaign	c. healthy to eat
_____ 4. nutritious	d. a set of rules and expectations
_____ 5. standards	e. unused materials
_____ 6. appearance	f. very surprising

3 **Listen.** Circle **T** for *True* or **F** for *False*. 028

1.	T	F	4.	T	F
2.	T	F	5.	T	F
3.	T	F	6.	T	F

4 **Listen again.** Correct the false statements. 029

____

____

____

5 **Write.** Use the words below to write sentences about ugly food.

1. challenge: ____

2. shocking: ____

3. standards: ____

GRAMMAR

***Going to*, *will* and present continuous: Talking about the future**

1. What **are you doing** tomorrow night?
2. I'**m going to eat** at the new Peruvian restaurant. Do you want to come?
3. I can't. I'**m visiting** my cousin tomorrow.
4. Why don't you both come?
5. a.) OK, I'**ll call** him and ask him. b.) I think he'**ll like** Peruvian food!
6. Great! This **is going to be** a fun night!

Use the present continuous and *going to* when future plans are made before the moment of speaking (examples 1, 2 and 3).

Use *will* when future plans are made at the moment of speaking (example 5a).

Finally, use *will* and *going to* to make future predictions (examples 5b and 6).

1 **Listen.** Write responses using *going to*, *will* or the present continuous. 030

1. ______________________________

2. ______________________________

3. ______________________________

4. ______________________________

5. ______________________________

6. ______________________________

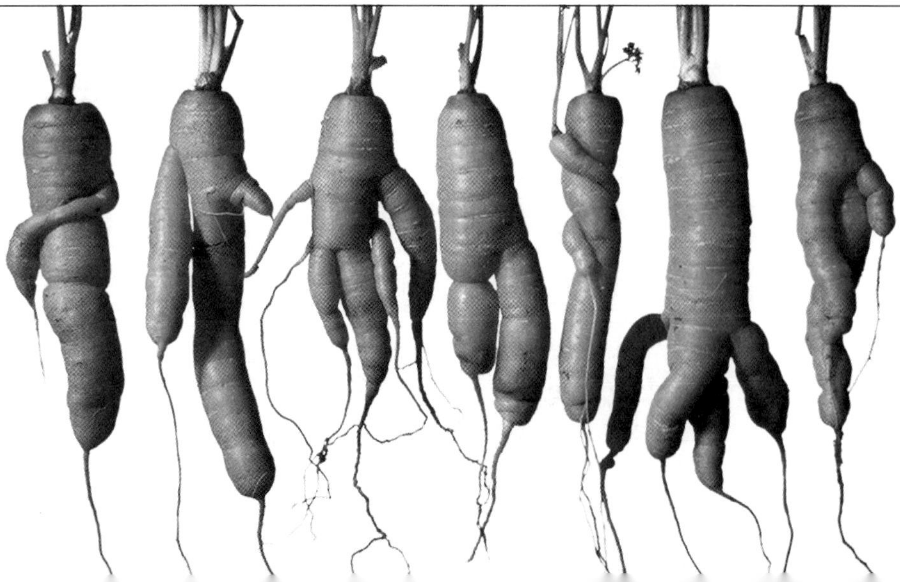

2 **Read each dialogue.** Fill in the blanks using the verb in brackets and *going to*, *will* or the present continuous.

Dialogue 1

Mika: What (do) ____________ with all those old carrots?

Ann: I'm (make) ____________ a fresh carrot soup.

Mika: Are those edible? Aren't you (throw away) ____________ ?

Ann: Of course not. They (make) ____________ a delicious and nutritious meal.

Dialogue 2

Suki: I'm (start) ____________ a campaign so that less food goes to waste.

Yun: How (do) ____________ that?

Suki: I'm (challenge) ____________ shops to sell food they normally throw away.

Yun: What if they (not do) ____________ it?

Suki: They will. I (make) ____________ posters for the shops. Also, I (teach) ____________ their consumers how to use produce that is not perfect.

3 **Look at the photos.** Write one sentence about each using *going to*, *will* or the present continuous.

1. ______________________________

2. ______________________________

1 **Listen and read.** Scan the text before you read. How many different numbers can you find? What do you think they represent? 031

Let's Stop Wasting Food!

How often do you or someone you know leave food on your plate? Does your family throw away food from the fridge because it's no longer fresh? If food waste is a problem in your home, think about what it's like worldwide.

About one-third of all food in the world is wasted. That's 1.2 billion metric tonnes of food. To give you an idea of how shocking that is, consider that the waste weighs as much as 200 million elephants! Among the waste, 45 per cent of fruit and vegetables is wasted, 35 per cent of seafood, and 30 per cent of cereal and grains. Milk products and meat are also wasted, but not as much. Most of this waste happens in North America and Europe, where about 100 kg of food per person is wasted each year. The United States alone, for example, wastes so much food that it could feed most of the country's hungry people for one year.

Food waste is indeed a big problem. It costs money and hurts the environment. But there are ways we can decrease the amount of food we reject and throw away. One way is to compost the food we do not eat. Composting is like recycling. Unwanted food breaks down and goes back into the soil to grow more fruit and vegetables.

- **1/3 of all food is wasted.**
- **In North America and Europe, 100 kg of food is wasted per person each year.**
- **Americans could feed 70% of the country's hungry people with the food they waste each year.**

We could also buy less at the supermarket and only fill our plates with what we know we will eat. We should take time to think about how much food we will actually eat. Another way to decrease food waste is to get involved with charity organisations and create campaigns that give food to people who often go hungry. Finally, give uneaten food to pets or farm animals. If we all make the decision to stop wasting food, we can make a difference!

2 **Read each statement.** Then tick **T** for *True* or **F** for *False*. Re-write the false statements to make them true.

	T	F
1. Food waste is a worldwide problem.	☐	☐
2. Cereal and grains are the most wasted foods in the world.	☐	☐
3. Americans feed all of their hungry with food they reject.	☐	☐
4. One way to decrease food waste is to compost it to grow more food.	☐	☐

____

____

3 **Read 'Let's Stop Wasting Food!' again.** List all the numbers you can find. Then write what each one represents.

Number	What does it represent?
1/3	amount of all food wasted worldwide

4 **You have read about worldwide food waste, as well as waste from school canteens.** Think about your eating habits at home, in restaurants and at school. Write what you are going to do to decrease food waste in your life.

____

____

____

____

GRAMMAR

Conditionals: Talking about cause and effect

***If* clause: present**	**Main clause: imperative**	
If you don't **finish** your dinner,	**save** the rest for tomorrow.	
***If* clause: present**	**Main clause: present**	
If the fruit **is** old,	we **use** it to make smoothies.	*This is always true/true now.*
***If* clause: present**	**Main clause: future**	
If you **put** less food on your plate,	you **will** not **waste** so much food.	*This will be true in the future.*

Conditional sentences have two clauses: The 'if' clause expresses a conditional using the present tense. The main clause expresses the result.

1 **Listen to the 'if' clauses.** Match the main clause to each. 032

1. _____
2. _____
3. _____
4. _____
5. _____

a. we eat it for a couple of days.
b. we buy them anyway.
c. I will help you make posters.
d. give the rest to the dog.
e. I will fry them.

2 **Write your own endings to the first three conditional clauses.** Then write three conditional sentences of your own.

1. If there is rotten food in our kitchen, ____________________
2. If I am served a food that looks strange, ____________________
3. If the vegetables are not fresh, ____________________
4. ____________________
5. ____________________
6. ____________________

3 **Read Ana's email and Paola's response.** Then pretend you are another one of her friends, Jorge or Eva, and write a response using conditionals.

To: Paola, Jorge, Eva **From:** Ana **Re:** My food campaign

Hi guys. I have made the decision to start a food campaign to feed people who have less food to eat than we do. I'm going to start by asking restaurants for food. I will need your help. If I give each of you a list of restaurants, will you go and talk to them? I want you to ask them to supply us with edible foods they plan to throw away. If we each visit two restaurants a week, we will have enough food to feed people in our neighbourhood.

We are going to need a kitchen and space to feed people, too. If you have any suggestions, I want to hear them. Also, if you know of anyone else who can help, please ask them to call or email me. This is going to be a challenge, but it will be worth it to help others.

Thanks! Talk to you soon!

Ana

To: Ana **From:** Paola **Re:** Ana's campaign

Ana, what a great idea! I'm excited to be involved in this campaign. If we ask my mum, she will probably let us use the school canteen. She is the head of the school, after all!

Paola

To: Ana **From:** ____________________ **Re:** Ana's campaign

____

____

____

____

____

WRITING

When we write to explain, we often describe the causes, or reasons, that bring about certain effects, or results. The causes are usually one or a series of actions or events.

To talk about causes and effects, we use phrases such as:

- as a result (of)
- because (of)
- due to
- for this reason/these reasons
- since
- that's why

1 Organise.

1. Your topic is *Why do people throw food away?* Look through the unit in your book as well as your workbook to find ideas about why people waste food. List at least three causes, or reasons, below.

Reasons/Causes for Wasting Food

2. Plan your writing. You'll need an introductory paragraph with a topic sentence that explains what your essay is about. Write your topic sentence here:

___

Next, you'll need at least two body paragraphs to talk about the causes of food waste.

Finally, you'll need a concluding paragraph. It will restate the topic sentence in different words.

2 Write.

1. Go to page 105 in your book. Re-read the model and writing prompt.
2. Write your first draft. Check for organisation, content, punctuation, capitalisation and spelling.
3. Write your final draft. Share it with your teacher and classmates.

Now I can ...

· talk about food waste.

☐ Yes, I can!
☐ I think I can.
☐ I need more practice.

Use words from the box to write two sentences about food waste.

fields	fresh	produce	reject	rotten	shocking	throw away	waste

1. ______________________________

2. ______________________________

· use *going to*, *will* and the present continuous to talk about the future.

☐ Yes, I can!
☐ I think I can.
☐ I need more practice.

Write one sentence about each photo using *going to*, *will* or the present continuous.

1. This evening, ______________________________.

2. Tomorrow morning, ______________________________.

· use conditionals to talk about cause and effect.

☐ Yes, I can!
☐ I think I can.
☐ I need more practice.

Write two conditional sentences about food or food waste.

If ________________, ________________.

If ________________, ________________.

· write a cause and effect essay about why people throw food away.

☐ Yes, I can!
☐ I think I can.
☐ I need more practice.

Write one cause of food waste that you did not write about in your essay.

____

____

____

YOU DECIDE **Choose an activity.** Go to page 95.

Units 5–6 Review

1 **Listen.** Answer the questions using the present perfect. You may use *never, ever, yet* or *already* as necessary. 033

1. Yes, I've been to Antarctica.
2. ______
3. ______
4. ______
5. ______

2 **Read.** Re-write the sentences using expressions of equality.

1. A baby elephant weighs 90 kg. (198 lb.) when it's born. That's how much an adult warthog weighs!
   When it's born, a baby elephant weighs as much as an adult warthog.
2. Warthogs are really ugly. So are slugs.
   ______
3. Both bats and moles are blind.
   ______
4. The hagfish and the anglerfish are both remarkable creatures.
   ______
5. Just like humans, fish need oxygen to live.
   ______
6. The deep sea is a harsh environment to exist in, just as the waters of the Antarctic are.
   ______

3 **Read the conversation about Sara and Jun's plans.** Choose the correct words to complete the sentences.

1. **Sara:** When _____ to the supermarket?
   a. do you go **b.** are you going **c.** you go
2. **Jun:** I _____ this afternoon, after school.
   a. go **b.** have gone **c.** am going
3. **Sara:** What _____ you buy there?
   a. will **b.** did **c.** do
4. **Jun:** I _____ fresh produce and supplies for soup.
   a. have bought **b.** am going to buy **c.** buy
5. **Sara:** Why _____ soup?
   a. do you make **b.** are you making **c.** did you make
6. **Jun:** My friends and I _____ each other to eat more nutritious meals.
   a. challenge **b.** challenged **c.** are challenging
7. **Sara:** Sounds great! I _____ the challenge with you!
   a. will do **b.** did **c.** have done
8. **Jun:** OK. We _____ to decrease waste by not throwing away so much food, too.
   a. try **b.** have tried **c.** are going to try
9. **Sara:** So, we _____ soup every day until it's gone!
   a. will eat **b.** ate **c.** have eaten

4 **Match the phrases to form logical sentences.**

_____ 1. If I start a food campaign,
_____ 2. If we all eat leftovers,
_____ 3. If you see produce that does not look fresh,
_____ 4. If you don't finish that pizza,
_____ 5. If the bananas are not the same size,
_____ 6. If we have potatoes tonight,
_____ 7. If I go out to eat,
_____ 8. If vegetables sit in the field,

a. buy it anyway.
b. we will boil and mash them.
c. most consumers reject them.
d. I take home what I don't finish.
e. they will become rotten.
f. we will throw away less food.
g. I hope you will be involved.
h. save the rest for tomorrow.

Unit 7

Art in the Open

1 Read the clues and fill in the puzzle.

Across

1. Some public art helps us ____ important events, like World War II.
2. Public art can also send messages about ____ issues.
3. Art can be about any ____ the artist is interested in.
4. Because of the painted houses on the hill in Mexico, colour ____ the neighbourhood.
5. The red polar bear on the ice in Iceland made people ____ that polar bears are in danger.
6. Sometimes art simply gives people ____ .
7. You can ____ art in museums as well as outside.

Down

8. You can see art in ____ ____ any time you wish.
9. Shannon Galpin ____ people what life is like in Afghanistan with her photographs.
10. Most statues stay in one place forever, but some public art displays are ____ .
11. Some public art ____ with political issues.
12. When we do not have to pay to see art, it is ____ .

2 **Match the words to their definitions.** Write the letter on the line.

______ 1. surround	a. for a short time
______ 2. take down	b. to bring something from the past to mind
______ 3. aware	c. to be all around a place
______ 4. temporary	d. areas open to everyone
______ 5. remember	e. to remove
______ 6. public space	f. knowing about something

3 **Listen.** Circle **T** for *True* or **F** for *False*. 034

1.	T	F	4.	T	F
2.	T	F	5.	T	F
3.	T	F	6.	T	F

4 **Listen again.** Correct the false statements. 035

____

____

____

5 **Look at the photos.** Choose two of the photos to write sentences about. Use at least one word from the box in each of your sentences.

free	joy	mural	pleasure	public spaces	surround	take down	temporary

____

____

____

GRAMMAR

Past simple vs. present perfect: Talking about the past

Have you **ever heard** of the Spanish artist, Jaume Plensa?
In 2000, he **designed** *Crown Fountain* in Chicago.
He **has created** dozens of sculptures throughout the world.
Plensa **has been** an artist ever since he **went** to art school in Barcelona.
Have you **seen** any of his work yet?

Use the present perfect for an action which happened in the past but can happen again in the future. The action may have happened only once, or it may have been repeated. It does not matter or it is not known exactly when the action happened.

Use the past simple when an action was completed in the past, and when you know when the action happened (see underlined examples above).

1 **Read the sentences.** Circle the correct verb form.

1. We **visited / have visited** art museums in Spain several times over the years.
2. We **have viewed / viewed** Jaume Plensa's work when we were there in 2014.
3. My cousin **has loved / loved** Plensa's work ever since she **has seen / saw** the sculpture at Millennium Park.
4. My friend **has expressed / expressed** herself with several art displays in public spaces in the past few years.
5. **Did they take down / Have they taken down** the temporary art displays yet?
6. **Have you shown / Did you show** your artwork to the gallery last week?
7. My cousin's sculptures **dealt with / have dealt with** various social issues over the years.

2 **Read.** Complete the sentences with the present perfect or past simple.

1. Jaume Plensa (study) ______________________ art at the Llotja School of Art and Design when he (be) ______________________ young.
2. In 2011, Plensa (show) ______________________ many of his works at an exhibition in England.
3. For years now, Plensa (be) ______________________ an art teacher at two big art schools.
4. Between 1996 and 2008, Plensa (work) ______________________ with others to create theatre and opera sets and costumes.
5. People throughout the world (enjoy) ______________________ Plensa's sculptures in public spaces.

3 **Listen.** Write responses in the present perfect or past simple. 036

1. Yes, I have travelled to Spain. I went there in 2013.
2. ____
3. ____
4. ____
5. ____
6. ____
7. ____
8. ____

1 **Before you read, look at the title and the photos.** What do you think the reading is about?

____

2 **Listen and read.** As you read, think about the main idea of the reading. 037

A Changing Community

Medellín, the second largest city in Colombia, used to not be a great place for children to grow up. Today, however, the people of Medellín are working together to make it a safer and more beautiful community. How are they doing this? Through art, of course!

The local government has given artists permission to paint murals on certain walls throughout the community. Artists are able to share their passion with others. They express themselves in their work. They also express a shared culture and shared values and memories. This builds respect among the residents.

The government's interest in the community helps the residents believe in the political system. To further support the residents of Medellín, the local government also supplies residents with brightly coloured paint to paint their houses. As residents plan and paint their homes together, they appreciate and understand each other more.

Another way Medellín is using art to improve their neighbourhoods is by giving children art classes. Community centres, such as Casa Morada, teach children how to paint and help them plan murals for public spaces. This is not only fun, but it has a serious side to it as well. It keeps children out of trouble and gives them a sense of pride in their neighbourhood.

Because of art, bright colours surround the community of Medellín. It gives the residents joy, pride and a sense of togetherness. As a result, Medellín is becoming a safer, more beautiful place.

3 **Read each statement.** Then tick **T** for *True* or **F** for *False*. Re-write the false statements to make them true.

	T	F
1. Public murals are illegal all over Medellín.	☐	☐
2. Art in the community of Medellín builds respect among residents.	☐	☐
3. Painting murals keeps children out of trouble in Medellín.	☐	☐
4. Residents of Medellín no longer believe in the local political system.	☐	☐

____

____

4 **Read 'A Changing Community' again.** Write the main idea below. Then add three details that support the main idea.

Main idea	Supporting details

5 **You have read about street art in Rio de Janiero and Medellín.** Write about how your community could benefit from community art.

____

____

____

____

GRAMMAR

Indefinite pronouns: Talking about people, places and things without giving details

I'm looking for **someone** to help me paint. Can **someone** help me paint this mural?	Use *someone, somewhere, something* to talk about a person, place or thing in positive statements. Also use in questions when you think you know the answer or are making an offer or request.
I can't find the large paintbrush **anywhere**. Is there **anything** else we can use? **Anyone** who tries can make art.	Use *anywhere, anything, anyone* in negative statements or questions when you are not sure of the answer. Also use in positive statements when 'any' means 'every'.
Nobody came to help me paint.	Use *nobody, no one, nowhere, nothing* to give statements a negative meaning.
I looked **everywhere** for the large paintbrush. Can **everyone** paint a part of the mural?	Use *everyone, everywhere, everything* in positive statements and questions.

Use indefinite pronouns to talk about people, places and things when the details are not known or not important.

1 **Listen to the statements and questions.** Circle the answer that should go where you hear a beep. 038

1. (anyone) / someone
2. somewhere / everywhere
3. anything / something
4. everything / anything
5. everyone / anyone
6. anyone / no one
7. anywhere / everywhere
8. Nobody / Everyone

2 **Read.** Complete the text with the correct indefinite pronoun.

(1) ______________ can paint a mural, but not (2) ______________ is an artist. Still, that should not stop (3) ______________ from trying to express him- or herself. There are lots of places people can paint on walls, but people can't paint just (4) ______________. Artists usually need permission to paint in public spaces. Without permission, there could be graffiti (5) ______________. (6) ______________, including artists, needs to respect public space. If you have (7) ______________ you think would be fun to paint in a public place, contact (8) ______________ in your local government to learn how to properly ask for permission.

3 **Read Cristiano's blog.** Then respond below. Try to use indefinite pronouns in your response.

Cristiano's Community Messenger

Is anyone interested in creating a mural for the local school with me? I really want to create something that represents our community. The school already has a few murals, but none of them say anything about who we really are.

I already have permission from the school head. So, the first thing I need is a group of volunteers. Not everyone on this project needs to be a part of the school. Anyone from the community is welcome.

Second, we need to plan on what the mural will show. Is there anything special we want it to say? And third, we need to decide where it will be. Is there somewhere in the school grounds you think would be perfect for a new mural? The canteen is an idea, but the old mural would have to be painted over, because, unlike other art forms, you can't take down a mural!

I would love to hear your thoughts and ideas. Thank you!

Cristiano

Lídia

What a great idea! I think everyone is going to be excited about this. I think the mural should show how we work together. Talk to you soon.

Rodolfo

I love this, too. It should be somewhere that everyone will see it.

WRITING

When we write to give instructions or explain a process, it's important to clearly outline and explain each step in order. It's often a good idea to make each step its own paragraph. To introduce each step, use words and phrases such as:

- First
- Second
- Then
- Next
- The next step
- After that
- At the end
- Finally
- The final step/thing

1 Organise.

1. Your topic is *How you would create a piece of public art for your school or community?* Look through the unit in your book, as well as this workbook, for ideas about the kind of art you want to create, what you want the subject to be, and where you want the art to be located. Then fill out the graphic organiser below. Include at least three steps for creating your art.

Kind of art:	Subject:	Location:
Steps: 1. 2. 3.		

2. Plan your writing. You'll need an introductory paragraph with a topic sentence that introduces your topic, including what kind of art you want to create, what the subject will be, and where it will be installed. Write your topic sentence here:

   ____

   Next, you'll need at least three paragraphs to explain each of the steps you will follow to create your public art.

2 Write.

1. Go to page 123 in your book. Re-read the model and writing prompt.
2. Write your first draft. Check for organisation, content, punctuation, capitalisation and spelling.
3. Check your final draft. Share it with your teacher and classmates.

Now I can ...

· talk about art in public spaces.

Use words from the box to write two sentences about public art. You may use the photos on this page for ideas.

- ☐ Yes, I can!
- ☐ I think I can.
- ☐ I need more practice.

aware	deals with	graffiti	joy	mural
respect	social topics	society	temporary	

1. ____________________
2. ____________________

· use the past simple and present perfect to talk about the past.

- ☐ Yes, I can!
- ☐ I think I can.
- ☐ I need more practice.

Write one question using the present perfect. Then write the answer to the question using the past simple.

1. ____________________
2. ____________________

· use indefinite pronouns to talk about people, places and things.

- ☐ Yes, I can!
- ☐ I think I can.
- ☐ I need more practice.

Fill in the blanks with the correct indefinite pronouns.

Suyin: Did you see ____________ walk by carrying a big paintbrush?

Ling: I did see ____________, but she wasn't holding ____________ in her hands.

Suyin: Thanks. Please tell ____________ to look ____________ for a big, blue paintbrush.

· write a process essay about how to create a piece of public art.

- ☐ Yes, I can!
- ☐ I think I can.
- ☐ I need more practice.

Write three sentences explaining how to draw a self-portrait.

____

____

____

YOU DECIDE **Choose an activity.** Go to page 96.

Unit 8

Don't Panic!

1 **Unscramble the words.** Then write the letters in the circles to complete the sentence below.

SCEPAE ___ (___) ___ ___ ___ ___

EABRETH ___ ___ ___ ___ (___) ___ ___

DWIRLFIE ___ ___ ___ ___ ___ ___ (___) ___

RDITSASE ___ (___) ___ ___ ___ ___ ___ ___

SEHAK ___ ___ ___ (___) (___)

LLCAUYREF (___) ___ ___ ___ ___ ___ ___ ___ (___)

ECLLOSAP (___) ___ (___) ___ ___ ___ ___ ___

SOURVRIV ___ ___ ___ ___ ___ ___ (___) ___

GWANINR ___ ___ ___ (___) ___ ___ ___

QUEAKRTHAE (___) ___ ___ ___ ___ ___ ___ ___ ___ ___

SFLMAE ___ ___ ___ ___ ___ (___)

Some disasters, like an avalanche, ___ ___ ___ ___ ___ ___ unexpectedly. Others, like ___ ___ ___ ___ ___ ___ ___ ___, give us some warning.

2 **Match each word to its definition.** Write the letter on the line.

_____ 1. terrible	a. with care
_____ 2. collapse	b. get out
_____ 3. warning	c. awful
_____ 4. carefully	d. fall on itself
_____ 5. escape	e. a sign

3 **Read.** Complete the sentences with words from the box.

breathe	**collapse**	**disasters**	**earthquakes**	**escape**
flames	**prevent**	**shaking**	**terrible**	

(1) ____Earthquakes____ are (2) ____________ events. There is nothing to do to (3) ____________ them, and they often cause other (4) ____________. For example, the (5) ____________ causes buildings to (6) ____________, which often starts electrical fires. The smoke makes it hard for people inside to (7) ____________. Also, it's often difficult to (8) ____________ from the hot (9) ____________.

4 **Listen.** Circle **T** for *True* or **F** for *False*. 039

1.	T	F	4.	T	F
2.	T	F	5.	T	F
3.	T	F			

5 **Listen again.** Correct the false statements. 040

____

____

6 **Write two sentences about natural disasters.** Use at least two words from the box in each sentence.

cyclone	**earthquake**	**predict**	**strike**	**survivors**	**terrible**	**unexpected**	**warning**	**wildfire**

1. ____

2. ____

GRAMMAR

Past simple vs. past continuous: Talking about the past

While I **was swimming** the other day, I **thought** about the dolphins that **saved** four lifeguards.
What **did** the dolphins **do** when they **knew** a shark was near? They **didn't swim** away. Instead, they **swam** around the lifeguards. They **were protecting** the lifeguards from harm.
What **were** the lifeguards **doing** in the water? They **were enjoying** a swim.
When the rescue boat **arrived**, the dolphins **were** still **keeping** the shark away from the lifeguards. The dolphins **stayed** close as the lifeguards **climbed** into the boat.

Use the past continuous to talk about an action that was already happening when another action began or happened. Use the past simple for that second action that began or happened.

To form the past continuous, use *was/were* + verb + *-ing*.

1 **Fill in the blanks.** Put the verbs in the correct tense: past simple or past continuous.

1. Jimmy Chin ________________ (hike) in the Himalayas when the weather unexpectedly ________________ (become) terrible.
2. Jimmy ________________ (ski) on a high mountain when an avalanche ________________ (strike) without warning.
3. The flames ________________ (burn) the building when the fire engine ________________ (come).
4. While we ________________ (live) in Chile, we ________________ (experience) an earthquake.
5. I suddenly ________________ (feel) the earth shake while I ________________ (read) my book.
6. The wildfire ________________ (start) while we ________________ (camp) in the forest.
7. ________________ (Do) the dolphins ________________ (chase) the shark away when they ________________ (see) it?

2 Read. Complete the sentences with the past simple or past continuous using the words and phrases from the box.

be	**be in trouble**	**drive**	**feel**	**live**	**happen**	**not pay attention**
play	**scream**	**see**	**stop**	**strike**	**take**	**talk**

When I (1) ____________ little, I (2) ____________ in a house on the edge of the forest. While I (3) ____________ outside with my little sister, I (4) ____________ smoke and flames at the top of the trees. Of course my sister (5) ____________ to what (6) ____________ . I knew we (7) ____________ , but I (8) ____________ brave. I carefully (9) ____________ my sister inside. My mum (10) ____________ on the phone, so I (11) ____________ , 'There is a wildfire coming!' My mum quickly (12) ____________ us to safety. Luckily, the firefighters (13) ____________ the fire before it (14) ____________ our house.

3 Listen. Write responses using the past simple or past continuous where needed. 041

1. *Jimmy Chin was brave when he was struck by an avalanche.*
2. ____________
3. ____________
4. ____________
5. ____________

1 **Before you read, look at the title and the photos.** What do you think the reading is about? Briefly write it here:

____

2 **Listen and read.** As you read, try to visualise, or see a picture in your mind of, the events the author describes. 042

TERROR Comes in Twos

Can you imagine being hit with two huge natural disasters at once? That's exactly what happened in northeastern Honshu, Japan's largest island, in March 2011. A powerful earthquake unexpectedly struck about 320 km. (200 mi.) north of Tokyo. It was followed by a terrible tsunami. Very few scientists predicted these disasters. Most people did not sense they were coming, so very few people prepared for them.

The earthquake was one of the strongest ever recorded. It shook the earth as far away as parts of Russia and China. It struck in the middle of the day, while many people were working or going to school. The earthquake collapsed buildings and caused a lot of terrible damage. People were terrified because they knew that soon a tsunami would hit. Many people went to higher ground or even climbed to the top of tall buildings to escape the tsunami.

About an hour later, waves 9 m. (or 30 ft.) high began hitting the land at 800 km. (500 mi.) per hour. Water poured over city walls and buildings, and destroyed more buildings. The waves pushed into the land about 5 km. (3 mi.) in from the shore. There was even one report that waves went as far ashore as 9.6 km. (6 mi.). The waves picked up everything in their path. As the waves moved back, they carried debris, including buildings, houses, boats and lorries back into the sea.

The Japanese government estimated that five million tonnes of debris was swept offshore. Some remains were left floating on the surface of the sea, but most of them sunk. The tsunami destroyed everything in its path and left many areas flooded. Its effects were eventually seen on the shores of Hawaii, the Aleutian Islands, the west coast of the United States, and, finally, Antarctica, where waves broke off the outer edge of the ice shelf.

3 **Read each statement.** Then tick **T** for *True* or **F** for *False*. Re-write the false statements to make them true.

	T	F
1. Two tsunamis hit Japan at the same time.	☐	☐
2. People did not expect a large earthquake.	☐	☐
3. After the earthquake, many people ran to high places.	☐	☐
4. Most of the debris from the disasters is floating in the sea.	☐	☐
5. Effects of the disasters were seen in China and Antarctica.	☐	☐

____

____

4 **Read 'Terror Comes in Twos' again.** Write down four images that you can visualise while reading the article. Then draw simple pictures of two of them.

Visualised images	Drawings
1.	
2.	
3.	
4.	

5 **You have read about an avalanche as well as an earthquake followed by a tsunami.** Briefly write about how the avalanche Jimmy Chin experienced and Japan's earthquake and tsunami are similar and how they are different.

____

____

____

GRAMMAR

Present perfect vs. present perfect continuous: Expressing the duration of activities

Mount St. Helens **has** not **erupted** since 1980. Mount St. Helens **has** not **erupted** for years.	Mount Etna **has been producing** smoke since early this morning. Mount Etna **has been producing** smoke for several hours.
She**'s climbed** many mountains since she was a teenager.	She**'s been climbing** mountains since she was 15. She and her father **have been climbing** mountains for seven years.
She**'s** always **known** she wanted to be a firefighter.	

To form present perfect continuous: *has/have* + *been* + verb + *ing*. Both the present perfect and present perfect continuous are used to talk about actions that started in the past and continue into the present. Both are often used with *since* and *for*. The present perfect continuous focuses on a continued activity. It is not used with verbs that describe a state of being, like *be*, *love* and *know*.

1 **Read.** Complete the text with the present perfect or present perfect continuous.

be climb hope love ski travel

My friend Aki (1) ____________ the outdoors since he was a child. He especially enjoys snow sports. For example, he (2) ____________ since he was five! He's even (3) ____________ icy mountains a few times! Right now, he's dogsledding in Iceland. He and his team (4) ____________ across the ice and snow for three days. I (5) ____________ to hear from him ever since he first arrived in Iceland a week ago. But he is in the middle of nowhere. Plus he (6) ____________ very busy!

2 **Listen to the questions.** Answer them using the present perfect and present perfect continuous. 043

1. I have liked winter sports since I was little.
2. ____________
3. ____________
4. ____________
5. ____________
6. ____________

3 **Read Carolina's blog.** Then respond below. Use the present perfect and present perfect continuous in your response.

Hello Readers!

Thanks for visiting my blog. I have been thinking a lot about the heroes in our lives. Do you have a hero? Maybe it is someone you have known for a long time. Maybe it is someone you do not know at all. Either way, it's important that we pay attention to our heroes and be grateful for how they help and inspire us.

One of my heroes is someone I have known since I was a baby. It's my Aunt Gabriela. Aunt Gabriela has been a firefighter for as long as I can remember. She has saved hundreds of lives. She is incredibly brave. She has faced all kinds of disasters. Not only has she run into the flames of burning homes and buildings to rescue people, she has also pulled survivors out of collapsed buildings after earthquakes. Once she even jumped out of a burning building with a dog in her arms! I would have been terrified, but not Aunt Gabriela. Aunt Gabriela, you are my hero!

Now, I want to hear from you. Please tell me about one of your heroes. What heroic things has he or she done?

Davi

My hero is my dad. He's taught me that it's important to take care of yourself. Since he's been running every morning, he has lost a lot of weight. I am so proud of him!

____

____

____

____

____

WRITING

When we write a narrative essay, we write a story about an experience or event. Like a story, the narrative should include a character or characters, setting, plot, climax and conclusion. In the final paragraph, we need to say why the story is important. For example, explain what the main character learnt or what the point or message of the story is.

1 Organise.

1. Your topic is *a true story about survival.* It could be about yourself, someone you know, or a famous person. Look through the unit in your book as well as this workbook for ideas for your narrative. If you are writing about a famous person, do some research on the Internet. Then fill out the table below.

Characters: *Who?*	
Setting: *When and where?*	
Plot: *Events and actions*	
Conflict/Climax: *What's the main problem?*	
Conclusion: *How did it end?*	
Message: *What's the point?*	

2. Plan your writing. You'll need an introductory paragraph with a topic sentence that introduces your topic and the person or people you are writing about. Write your topic sentence here:

____

3. Next, you'll need a couple of paragraphs to explain the setting, plot, conflict and climax. The final paragraph will include the conclusion, or what happened in the end, and the message or point you want to share about the story.

19 Write.

1. Go to page 139 in your book. Re-read the model and writing prompt.
2. Write your first draft. Check for organisation, content, punctuation, capitalisation and spelling.
3. Check your final draft. Share it with your teacher and classmates.

Now I can ...

· talk about being prepared in the face of disaster.

☐ Yes, I can!
☐ I think I can.
☐ I need more practice.

Use words from the box to write two sentences about natural disasters. You may use the photos on this page for ideas.

collapse	**cyclone**	**earthquake**	**escape**	**pay attention to**	**predict**	**shake**	**strike**	**terrible**	**wildfire**

1. ______________________________

2. ______________________________

· use the past simple and past continuous to talk about the past.

☐ Yes, I can!
☐ I think I can.
☐ I need more practice.

Put the verbs in the past simple and past continuous.

While we ______________ (camp), a wildfire ______________ (start) in the forest. We ______________ (be) terrified. I ______________ (still scream) after we ______________ (escape) the flames.

· use the present perfect and present perfect continuous to talk about the duration of activities.

☐ Yes, I can!
☐ I think I can.
☐ I need more practice.

Put the verbs in the present perfect and present perfect continuous.

My uncle ______________ (chase) storms, like tornadoes and cyclones, ever since he survived a terrible tornado as a young man. He ______________ (photograph) hundreds of disasters all over the world. He ______________ (be) in terrible trouble many times.

· write a narrative essay about a survival story.

☐ Yes, I can!
☐ I think I can.
☐ I need more practice.

Think about a survival story different from the one you wrote earlier. It could be about an animal or a person. In a few sentences, write who the story is about, what happened, and what the point of the story is.

____

____

____

YOU DECIDE **Choose an activity.** Go to page 96.

Units 7–8 Review

1 Read the sentences below. Choose the correct answer.

1. _____ of the Spanish artist, Joan Miró?
   a. Has you ever heard **b.** Did you ever heard **c.** Have you ever heard

2. He _____ a painter and sculptor who _____ in 1983.
   a. was **b.** have been **c.** has been
   a. has died **b.** died **c.** was dying

3. I _____ my studio with images of his work after I _____ his paintings at a museum last year.
   a. surround **b.** have surrounded **c.** surrounded
   a. have viewed **b.** viewed **c.** was viewing

4. I _____ down images of other artists yet, but I am going to.
   a. haven't taken **b.** hasn't taken **c.** did not took

5. My mother _____ Miró since she _____ young, too.
   a. loved **b.** was loving **c.** has loved
   a. has been **b.** was **c.** being

6. My mum _____ herself through art over the last several years, just like I have.
   a. expresses **b.** expressed **c.** has expressed

7. She _____ some of her works in a gallery in 2001.
   a. showed **b.** is showing **c.** has shown

8. We _____ each other's work, even though we have different styles.
   a. respecting **b.** have respected **c.** respected

2 Complete the text with the correct indefinite pronoun.

anything	anywhere	everyone	everywhere	no one	someone	something

Art does not have to be serious, or deal with a social topic. It can be almost (1) ____anything____. Even (2) ________________ fun. The important thing is that the artist expresses him- or herself. Perhaps (3) ________________ will understand what the artist is trying to say, but that's OK.

Not (4) ________________ likes art, but I happen to be (5) ________________ who does. I get such joy out of seeing paintings in galleries or a sculpture in a public space. I love to view art just about (6) ________________, really. If art were (7) ________________ and surrounded me, I would be happy.

3 **Read.** Choose the correct answer to express the past.

While I (1) ____ in Japan, I (2) ____ a typhoon. Typhoons never (3) ____ where I (4) ____ up, so the storm (5) ____ unexpected and terrifying. I (6) ____ my teeth when the rain (7) ____ . I (8) ____ much attention to it until the windows (9) ____ to shake. Wind and water (10) ____ my building so hard I (11) ____ the windows would break. When I (12) ____ brave enough, I carefully (13) ____ out the window. Water (14) ____ everywhere. I eventually fell asleep to the sound of the wind and water. While I (15) ____ , the storm died down and I suddenly (16) ____ up to silence.

1.	a. been living	b. was living	c. have lived
2.	a. experienced	b. have experienced	c. was experiencing
3.	a. has struck	b. were striking	c. struck
4.	a. have grown	b. grew	c. am growing
5.	a. was	b. has been	c. is being
6.	a. brushed	b. have brushed	c. was brushing
7.	a. have started	b. started	c. starting
8.	a. haven't paid	b. haven't been paying	c. didn't pay
9.	a. began	b. beginning	c. have begun
10.	a. were hitting	b. have hit	c. are hitting
11.	a. have thought	b. thought	c. am thinking
12.	a. have felt	b. have feeling	c. felt
13.	a. was looking	b. looked	c. have looked
14.	a. was rushing	b. has been rushing	c. has rushed
15.	a. have slept	b. slept	c. was sleeping
16.	a. was waking	b. woke	c. have woken

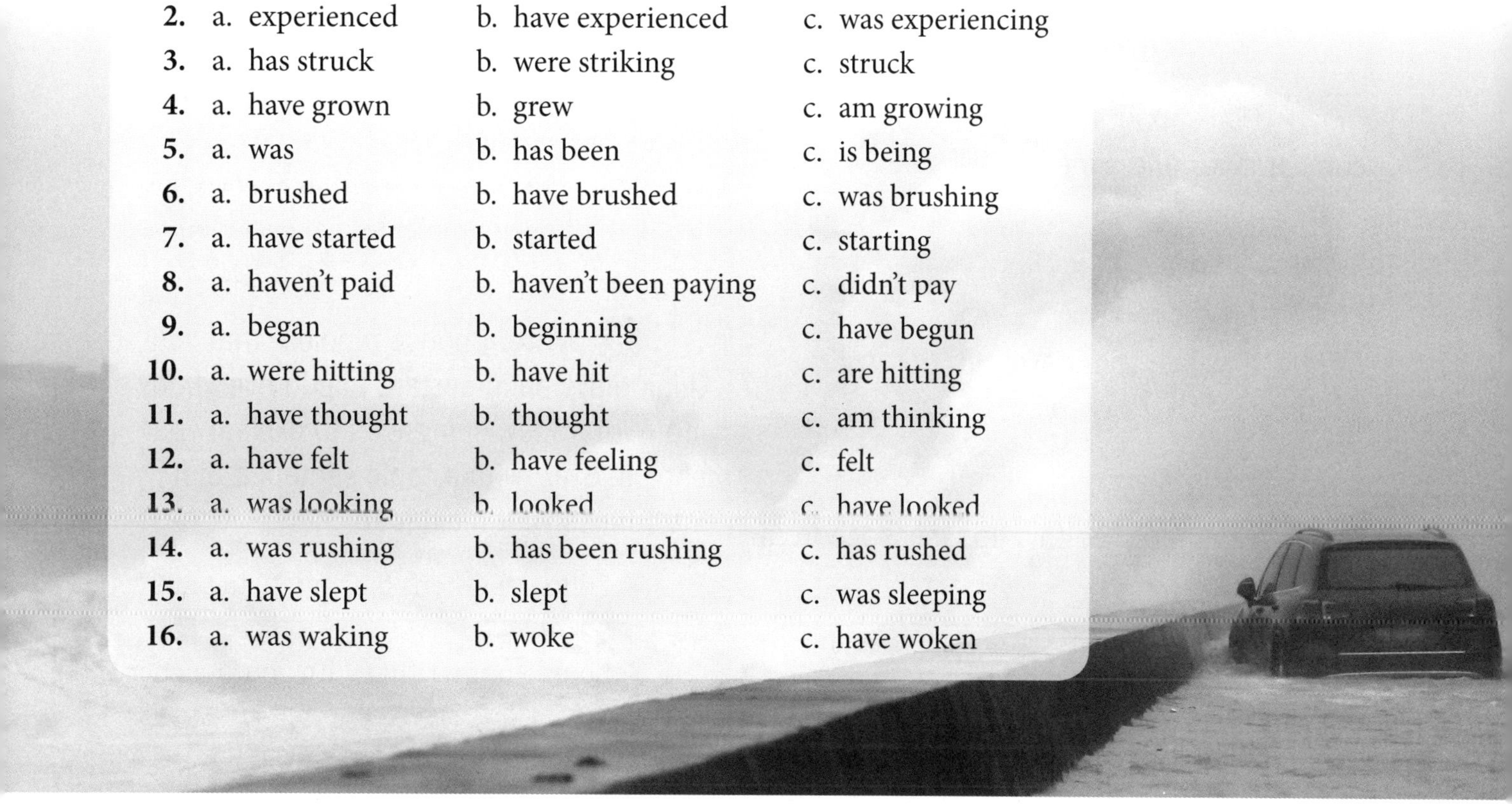

4 **Listen to the questions.** Answer them using the present perfect and present perfect continuous. 044

1. I have loved outdoor sports since I was little.

2. ______________________________

3. ______________________________

4. ______________________________

5. ______________________________

6. ______________________________

YOU DECIDE Choose an activity. Unit 1

☐ **1** Describe a colour without saying what the colour is. Use words from the list. Take turns asking a classmate to guess the colour.

common	**danger**	**flag**
nervous	**ordinary**	**relaxed**
royalty	**sign**	**warning**
wedding		

☐ **2** Talk about the following topics using comparatives and superlatives.

1. white wedding dress / red wedding dress / good
2. blue / purple / common
3. the colour red / the colour green / relaxed
4. bright colours / dark colours / pretty

☐ **3** You received this text message from a friend.

> I need help redecorating my room. I want to paint the wall next to my bed a different colour from the other walls. What colour should it be? Also, what should I put on the other walls?

Respond with at least three sentences. Make sure you use the definite article *the* and the indefinite article *a*.

☐ **4** **Work in pairs.** Talk about a picture or image in your classroom. Each person should:

- comment on the colours or design of the picture
- express what he or she likes or dislikes about the picture
- ask his or her partner one question about the picture
- practise the conversation with his or her partner
- act out the conversation in class, or use a phone or tablet to make a video.

☐ **5** **Write.** Choose a colour that you think plays an important role in everybody's life. Write a few sentences to explain your choice. Start with a topic sentence that introduces your main idea.

- Follow the steps on page 10 to plan your writing.
- Share your writing with your teacher and classmates.

☐ **6** This is part of an email you received from an American friend.

> *At school, we are working on a project about the importance of colours in different cultures. What's an important colour in your culture? Is it connected to a festival or a holiday? Why?*

Respond to the email. Write at least 100 words.

YOU DECIDE Choose an activity. Unit 2

☐ **1** Describe ways that you and your body fight disease and poor health. Use words from the list. Take turns with a classmate.

antibiotics	**bacteria**	**emotion**
illness	**immune system**	**positive**
protect	**rest**	**treat**
vaccinations		

☐ **2** Talk about your sleeping habits. Use adverbs that say *How often*, such as *always, occasionally, often, sometimes* and *rarely*. Also use adverbs that say *How*, such as *well, poorly, calmly*, etc.
Use these questions to get started:

- How often do you go to bed early?
- How do you feel when you don't get enough sleep?

☐ **3** Your mum left this note for you.

> *You have an early doctor's appointment in the morning. I don't want you to play video games tonight. You need to go to bed early.*
> *Love, Mum*

Respond and tell her how you feel about going to the doctor, not playing video games, and going to bed early. Use *make* or *makes* + an adjective in your response.

☐ **4** **Work in pairs.** Interview a classmate about what makes him or her stressed and what he or she does to relax.

- Prepare five questions.
- Assign roles.
- Practise the conversation.
- Swap roles.
- Act out the interviews in class, or use a phone or tablet to make a video.

☐ **5** Write a classification essay about the positive effects of sleep. Make sure you divide the effects into categories that you support with examples.

- Follow the steps on page 20 to plan your writing.
- Share your writing with your teacher and classmates.

☐ **6** This is part of a letter from your friend, Josh, in America.

> *I almost always eat three meals a day and only have healthy snacks, like apples and carrots. I ride my bike to school. Also, I often go to bed early so I am ready for the next day. Tell me about you. What do you do to make sure both your mind and body are healthy?*

Respond to the letter. Write at least 100 words.

YOU DECIDE Choose an activity. Unit 3

☐ **1** Describe ways that the Internet affects our lives. Use words from the list. Take turns with a classmate.

access	**communicate**	**extend**
focus	**improve**	**information**
instant	**interfere**	**rely on**
social media		

☐ **2** Talk about rules for using social media and creating accounts on the Internet. Use modals of obligation (*have to/must*), advice (*should/shouldn't*), and permission (*can/may/can't*).

Use these topics to get started:

- How to treat online friends
- Usernames and passwords

☐ **3** You and your friend are studying in the library. He just passed this note to you:

> *I just saw a video of a six-foot lizard stopping traffic on the motorway! It even tried to swallow a car!*

Respond to and express what you do and don't believe with *must*, *might* and *can't*.

☐ **4** **Work in pairs.** Interview cyborg anthropologist Amber Case.

- Research Amber Case on the Internet and in your student's book.
- Prepare five questions.
- Assign roles.
- Practise the interview.
- Act out the interview in class, or use a phone or tablet to make a video.

☐ **5** Write an opinion essay about whether or not we should have robots working in our homes. Make sure you support your opinion with facts.

- Follow the steps on page 32 to plan your writing.
- Share your writing with your teacher and classmates.

☐ **6** This is part of a blog you are following.

> We all rely on digital technology so much in our lives; I wonder if we can live without it? I suppose it depends on where we are and what we are doing. Readers around the world, tell me about the use of digital technology in your culture. Are there any you can't live without? Why or why not?

Respond to the blog. Write at least 100 words.

YOU DECIDE Choose an activity. Unit 4

☐ **1** Describe what underwater explorers do and what their journeys are like. Use words from the list. Take turns with a classmate.

destination	**expedition**	**find out**
identify	**look for**	**messages**
preparation	**reach**	**remains**
set off	**transmit**	

☐ **2** Read the passage below. Then retell it using *used to, would* or *use to* with the correct form of the underlined verbs.

> Long ago, explorers <u>dreamt</u> of going on long underwater expeditions, but they weren't sure it was possible. Similarly, there was a time when people <u>thought</u> space travel was a crazy idea. Did people <u>think</u> it was possible? Some <u>believed</u> it was, but not in their lifetime.

☐ **3** This is part of an email you received from a friend who is on holiday.

> I finally went on my first plane ride. I was scared when the engine turned on. Then my dad gave me my book. I read it and it helped me relax. I felt so happy when we finally reached our destination.

Respond with three sentences about a time you were scared to do something. Use the past simple.

☐ **4** **Work in pairs.** Interview an underwater explorer such as Katy Croff Bell or Robert Ballard.

- Research the explorer on the Internet.
- Prepare five questions.
- Assign roles.
- Practise the interview.
- Act out the interview in class, or use a phone or tablet to make a video.

☐ **5** Write a contrast essay about a mythical place. Some ideas are Atlantis and Shangri-La. Make sure you use phrases that express contrast like *although*, *at the same time*, and *however.*

- Follow the steps on page 42 to plan your writing.
- Share your writing with your teacher and classmates.

☐ **6** This is part of an email you received from an Australian friend.

> We are doing a project at school about important ancient remains around the world. Tell me about an ancient structure in your country. How old is it? Is it natural or man-made?

Respond to the email. Write at least 100 words.

YOU DECIDE Choose an activity. Unit 5

☐ **1** Describe one creature that lives in a very cold place, and one that lives in a very hot place. Use words from the list. Take turns with a classmate.

adapt	**conditions**	**environment**
exist	**handle**	**harsh**
rare	**remarkable**	**thrive**
tolerate	**typical**	

☐ **2** Read the passage below. Then retell it by putting the verbs in the present perfect.

> My uncle visited many extreme environments. He went to Antarctica and a couple of destinations in Russia. He also travelled to very hot places like the Lut Desert in Iran and Death Valley in the United States. He always likes to challenge himself. He wondered if he could handle a variety of harsh conditions. Now he knows he can!

☐ **3** You received this text message from a friend.

> Have you ever seen a proboscis monkey? It is a bizarre animal. Its nose is as long as a banana! But it can swim as fast as a crocodile. Even faster sometimes! That's remarkable!

Respond with your opinion about another remarkable animal. Use *as* ... *as* to make at least two comparisons.

☐ **4** **Work in pairs.** Have a conversation about bizarre animals or extreme environments. Each person should:

- express something about the topic
- ask his or her partner two questions about the topic
- practise the conversation with his or her partner
- act out the conversation in class, or use a phone or tablet to make a video.

☐ **5** Write a persuasive essay about an animal that should be your new school mascot. Make sure you support your reasons with facts.

- Follow the steps on page 54 to plan your writing.
- Share your writing with your teacher and classmates.

☐ **6** This is part of a letter you received from your American pen friend.

> *For my homework project I have to write about the variety of environments in different countries. What's the landscape and weather like in your country? Are there mountains, deserts, or a big body of water? Is it hot or cold, or maybe both?*

Respond to the letter. Write at least 100 words.

YOU DECIDE Choose an activity. Unit 6

☐ **1** Describe some reasons that food is wasted. Use words from the list. Take turns with a classmate.

appearance	**consumers**	**edible**
fields	**fresh**	**landfill**
nutritious	**produce**	**reject**
rotten	**supermarket**	

☐ **2** Read the steps for making tomato soup.

1. Go to the supermarket.
2. Buy some garlic, onions and tomatoes.
3. Chop the vegetables.
4. Fry them in oil for a few minutes.
5. Add water and spices.
6. Bring it to a boil, and then let it simmer for 40 minutes.

Retell the process for making tomato soup as something you are planning on doing. Use *going to*, *will* and the present continuous.

☐ **3** You received this text message from a friend.

> If I start a campaign to educate our friends about healthy foods, would you help me? I'm not sure if we should promote healthy foods only, tell children about how bad junk food is, or both. What do you think?

Respond with your opinion. Use at least one conditional sentence in your response.

☐ **4** **Work in pairs.** Interview a famous chef.

- Research a famous chef on the Internet.
- Prepare five questions.
- Assign roles.
- Practise the interview.
- Act out the interview in class, or use a phone or tablet to make a video.

☐ **5** Write a cause-and-effect essay that explains why people need to eat a healthy, well-balanced diet. Make sure you discuss the causes that bring about certain results.

- Follow the steps on page 64 to plan your writing. You may need to do some research on the Internet as well.
- Share your writing with your teacher and classmates.

☐ **6** This is part of a food blog you have been following.

> *For our food blog, we are collecting information about people's eating habits around the world. Please tell me about what people like to eat in your country. Do you have three meals a day? What times? Do you often go out or do you eat at home? Who do you eat with?*

Respond to the questions in the blog. Write at least 100 words.

YOU DECIDE Choose an activity. Units 7–8

☐ **1** With a classmate, discuss how art has helped you or others. Use words from the list. Also use the past simple and present perfect.

aware	**deals with**	**express oneself**
pleasure	**remember**	**respect**
social topics	**society**	**view**

☐ **2** You received this email from your friend who is planning a party.

> I want to plan something fun for the block party. My parents gave us permission to design and draw artwork in chalk on the driveway. Do you think everyone would like that? What should the subject be? Do you have any other ideas for the party?

Respond. Use some indefinite pronouns in your response.

☐ **3** Write an essay that explains how you would plan a trip to view art in or near your hometown. Explain each step in order.

- Follow the steps on page 76 to plan your writing. Replace the categories in the graphic organiser with: *Where? Who?* and *How will you get there?*
- Share your writing with the class.

☐ **4** This is part of a news story you read.

> **Bugs Cover Gallery Walls**
>
> *Artist Jennifer Angus has decorated the walls of the local museum with bugs! She used thousands of bugs to create designs that look like wallpaper. She wants viewers to think about taking better care of our environment and to get involved with campaigns that protect the world's rain forests.*

Write an essay about a social or political issue from your culture and how it has been or could be expressed in art. Write at least 100 words.

☐ **1** **Work in pairs.** Interview a classmate about surviving a natural disaster. Use words from the list.

be in trouble	**breathe**	**escape**
eventually	**shake**	**strike**
terrible	**terrified**	**unexpected**

- Choose a disaster.
- Prepare five questions. Use the simple past and past continuous.
- Assign roles.
- Practise the interview.
- Act it out in class, or make a video.

☐ **2** Talk about someone you know who likes outdoor activities. Use the present perfect (*has played*) and the present perfect continuous (*has been playing*). Use these questions to get started:

- How many times has your friend done this activity?
- How long has your friend been doing this activity?

☐ **3** Write a narrative essay about a true hero who saved people from a disaster. Make sure you say what the point of the story is.

- Follow the steps on page 86 to plan your writing.
- Share your writing with your teacher and classmates.

☐ **4** This is part of an email you received from a Canadian pen friend.

> There was another avalanche in the mountains! My brother and I had just been snowboarding there the day before. How scary! What kinds of natural disasters happen where you live?

Respond to the email. Write at least 100 words.